Babylon in Greek Literature

Demirel Miholic

ABSTRACT

This book delves into the captivating allure of Babylon within the Greek imaginaire, serving as a cultural and literary crossroads during the imperial period. Spanning from the fifth century BCE to the third/fourth century CE, the study analyzes an array of sources, including historiographies, biographies, magico-medical texts, comic dialogues, and the ancient novel. Babylon is examined through different lenses, revealing the Greeks' diverse perceptions of this legendary city.

The Greeks revered Babylon as a symbol of cultural hybridity, where diverse traditions and knowledge intermingled. The city's allure also lay in its capacity to evoke both historical and scientific curiosity, while at the same time sparking the magical and fictional imagination. Within the literary context, Babylon emerged as a space of esoteric wisdom, holding the secrets of ancient knowledge that captured the minds of the learned.

On the contrary, Babylon was not without its darker aspects, as it was often sensationalized as a dangerous and mysterious place. The Greeks found fascination in the untamed and enigmatic reputation of the city, which led to tales of wonder and peril that reverberated throughout the ancient world.

The book explores how these two intertwined strands of the Greek imagination—enigmatic wisdom and sensationalized danger—converged and manifested themselves in the form of the ancient novel. Through a comprehensive analysis of various literary works, the study uncovers how Babylon became a recurring theme in these narratives, wherein characters embarked on transformative journeys, seeking both profound wisdom and confronting perilous encounters.

Ultimately, "Babylon in Greek Literature" illuminates the complexities of this ancient city's representation in the Greek psyche. It reveals how Babylon, as a literary motif, mirrored the multifaceted nature of the

Greek society, blending exoticism and enchantment with intellectual pursuit and cautionary tales. This book contributes to a deeper understanding of the cultural exchange between the Greeks and the captivating allure of Babylon as a timeless symbol of human imagination.

ACKNOWLEDGEMENTS

The completion of this book would not have been possible without the support, guidance, and encouragement of several individuals and institutions. I express my heartfelt gratitude to all those who contributed to this endeavor.

First and foremost, I extend my sincere appreciation to my supervisor and academic mentor, [Supervisor's Name], for their invaluable guidance, insightful feedback, and unwavering support throughout the research process. Their expertise and encouragement were instrumental in shaping the direction of this study.

I extend my thanks to the numerous scholars, researchers, and experts in the field of Greek literature, whose works laid the foundation for this study. Their groundbreaking research has been indispensable in shaping the ideas presented in this book.

I also extend my appreciation to the participants of any interviews or surveys conducted during the research, as well as any individuals who assisted with the sourcing and interpretation of ancient texts and manuscripts. Their contributions added depth and authenticity to the findings.

Furthermore, I am grateful to my friends and family for their unwavering support and understanding during this intense academic journey. Their encouragement and belief in my abilities were constant sources of motivation.

Lastly, I would like to express my gratitude to the readers and scholars who will engage with this book. I hope that this work will add to the body of knowledge and inspire further exploration into the fascinating realm of Babylon in Greek literature.

Thank you all for being a part of this journey and for enriching my life with your presence and support.

TABLE OF CONTENTS

<u>ABBREVIATIONS</u>

BM	British Museum.
BNJ	Brill's New Jacoby.
BNP	Brill's New Pauly.
FGrHist	Die Fragmente der Griechischen Historiker.
LSJ	Liddell and Scott revised by Jones.
POxy	Papyrus Oxyrhynchus.

<u>INTRODUCTION</u>

"What have the Romans ever done for us?"
- Monty Python, *Life of Brian* (1979)

The famous comedy sketch from Monty Python's Life of Brian highlights the numerous social, intellectual and political facets which modern western civilisation can trace back to the Romans. While Rome and Greece are traditionally seen as the roots of the "West" in the popular imagination, many core elements of our culture actually have roots in Babylon and Mesopotamia. Over two millennia before the birth of the Roman Empire, Babylon was a thriving hub of intellectual activity. The scribal tradition of ancient Mesopotamia predates the earliest records of the Greek alphabet by over a millennium.[1] Amongst the oldest surviving literary works are the Sumerian poems ascribed to Enheduana, dating to over four thousand years ago, and the *Epic of Gilgamesh*, composed nearly four thousand years ago. Other early Mesopotamian writings included cosmological and celestial observations as Babylon was at the centre of ancient scientific discovery. From astrology/ astronomy, mathematics and medicine, much of western science is indebted to ancient Mesopotamia. The sexagesimal (a numeral system with sixty as its base) originated in Mesopotamia during the third millennium BCE and continues to be used as the standard unit for time and angles.

Today Babylon is mostly associated with the legendary Hanging Garden despite the absence of archaeological evidence for its existence. For over two millennia the Hanging Garden has captivated audiences and contributed towards the mysticism and lore of the city. Babylon has had to contend with a reputation as a sensual and corrupt city in the modern western imagination, largely owing to its depiction in the Bible, especially the *Book of Daniel*.[2] For centuries Babylon was

---

[1] Shortly after 3500 BCE Sumerians in southern Mesopotamia began to develop a system of writing, whereas the earliest evidence for the Greek alphabet is the Linear B tablet, dating to the second millennia BCE. See Verbrugghe & Wickersham (2001), 2-6 for a summary languages and scripts of ancient Mesopotamia.

[2] Whilst Greek texts similarly presented Babylon as a sensationalised and licentious space, the prevalence of this characterisation in the European imagination was due rather to Babylon's depiction in the Bible. For the general population of Medieval and Early-Modern Europe, the Bible far exceeded the accessibility of Greek literature.

exclusively viewed through a non-Mesopotamian lens since cuneiform script was not deciphered until the nineteenth century, resulting in numerous orientalist clichés and misconceptions of Babylon overshadowing the city's intellectual achievements. This thesis addresses the origins of European cultures writing about their Near Eastern neighbours, specifically exploring impressions of Babylon in Greek literature, how on one hand it was presented as a space of esoteric wisdom, and on the other, a dangerous and sensationalised space, and how these two strands of the imagination combined in the form of the ancient novel.

Literary survey

There are currently few studies dedicated to Graeco-Babylonian relations, especially in the post-Hellenistic period. The current scholarship tends to focus more-broadly on Greece and Mesopotamia, rather than specifically Babylon. An exception to this is Kathryn Stevens' recent monograph which provides a comprehensive study focusing on the cultural interaction between Greece and Babylon.[3] Stevens concentrates on the transfer of knowledge and cross-cultural exchange between the regions, drawing upon cuneiform and Greek material and argues that there are significant parallels between Greek and Babylonian intellectual culture owing to their incorporation into the same Hellenistic imperial system.

The majority of scholarship on Greece and Mesopotamia similarly focuses on the transmission of knowledge between the regions. There are numerous studies exploring the relationship between Greek and Near-Eastern literature, specifically the recurring patterns and motifs which suggests transmission between cultures. *The Romance between Greece and the Near East* edited by Tim Whitmarsh and Stuart Thomson, contains a collection of essays assessing contact zones between the Greco-Roman world and the Near East.[4] The volume focuses specifically on prose fiction, and provides an intercultural perspective, considering the influence of Egyptian, Mesopotamian and Persian literature in the Graeco-Roman world. Johannes Haubold provides a comparative literary study of Greek and Mesopotamian literature, including comparing Homer and *Gilgamesh*, arguing that

---

[3] Stevens (2019).
[4] Whitmarsh and Thomson (2013).

the literature of these cultures gradually became entwined.[5] Tim Whitmarsh's *Dirty Love* similarly considers the relationship between Greek and near-eastern literature, focusing specifically on the emergence of the Greek novel/ romance.[6] Whilst, like these scholars, I briefly touch upon Mesopotamian scientific and literary influences on Greek culture/ society in my discussion of the Mesopotamian influence over Graeco-Roman garden-design and legislation outlawing astrologers, I am primarily interested in the literary depiction of Babylon and the role the city played in the Greek imaginaire.

There is a plethora of scholarship focusing on the Greek depiction of the Achaemenid Empire and Achaemenid court, which occasionally incorporates Babylon into the discussion. These studies tend to adopt a historical approach, considering the historicity of the Greek literary and material representation of their eastern neighbours and tend to address Greek sources dating to the Classical period.[7] It was during this period the Greek literary genre of *Persica* emerged, which focused on the history and culture of the Persian Empire. This coincided with the Graeco-Persian wars which increased the contact between Greece and Mesopotamia. Many authors of *Persica* were from Asia Minor, which was under the intermittent control of the Achaemenid Empire. These authors attempted to understand their eastern neighbours (and occasional rulers), but also sought to establish a Greek identity distinct from the 'Other'.[8] Edward Saïd's seminal study traces the origins of Orientalism to the Greek depiction of the Achaemenids, specifically Aeschylus' *Persians*, whilst Heleen Sancisi-Weerdenburg argues that Ctesias was the first proponent of Orientalism.[9]

Ctesias' *Persica* is a central text in this thesis, and the past two decades has seen an increasing amount of scholarship on the text, including multiple

---

[5] Haubold (2013a).
[6] Whitmarsh (2018).
[7] See Morgan (2016), 1-17 for an overview on the current scholarship.
[8] Sancisi-Weerdenburg (1987b), fn. 15; Hall (1989); Llewellyn-Jones and Robson (2010), 55. Cf. Gruen (2011) who rejects typical view that Greeks defined themselves in contrast to foreign peoples and the demonising the other, arguing that Greek sources are more complex and nuanced in their presentation of foreigners. See also Morgan (2016), 126-129 for an overview on scholarship addressing the Greek invention of the 'Other'.
[9] Said (1978), 56; Sancisi-Weerdenburg (1987a).

commentaries.[10] The scholarship on Ctesias' *Persica* tends to focus on how to define the text's genre, with the majority arguing that it is neither a pure history nor a pure romance, but instead a hybrid of the two.[11] It is difficult to determine how Ctesias envisioned his work due to the little which survives from Ctesias himself, and fragments and epitomes often reflect the interests of the authors who cite or summarise them, rather than the original work.[12] There has been much historiographical discussion on the personal objectives of the authors transmitting Ctesias' text, and how this may have influenced their representation of Ctesias.[13] Rather than enter the debate on the historicity of Ctesias' *Persica* and the complexities regarding its transmission, I instead consider Ctesias' influence on Greek views towards Babylon.[14]

Whilst the Graeco-Persian wars increased contact between Greece and Mesopotamia, the intermingling of cultures was further enhanced following the conquests of Alexander of Macedon and the subsequent Hellenistic kingdoms. Babylon, and all of Mesopotamia, was incorporated into the Seleucid Empire. In order to enhance the legitimacy of their rule, early Seleucid rulers assimilated themselves with native customs and people, marrying members of prominent local families and affiliating themselves with the Babylonian king Nebuchadnezzar, performing symbolic acts, such as Antiochus III being presented with the purple robe of Nebuchadnezzar during a visit to Babylon.[15] Nebuchadnezzar was a central figure in Berossus' *Babyloniaka,* which is the only surviving example of a Babylonian scholar writing in Greek. Berossus is an example of cultural hybridity of the period, which saw the development of local histories: texts written by non-Greeks about their region for a Greek audience. Hence, multiple studies on Berossus compare him to his contemporary Mantheo, who was likewise a native priest writing a local history

---

[10] Lenfant (2004); Llewellyn-Jones & Robson (2010); Stronk (2010).
[11] Marincola (1997), 22; Briant (2002), 272; Stronk (2004-5), pp; Stronk (2007), 43-55; Whitmarsh (2008), 2; Llewellyn-Jones & Robson (2010), 68-80; Wieshöfer (2013), 137-141; Whitmarsh (2018), 43-5.
[12] See Brunt (1980), 494; Stronk (2007), 49; Whitmarsh (2018), 45.
[13] See Bingwood (1980); Stronk (2004-5); Stronk (2007), 26-37; Llewellyn-Jones & Robson (2010), 34-5; Whitmarsh (2018), 45.
[14] Following Wiesehöfer (2013) 137 suggestion that instead of using Ctesias as a source for the reconstruction of the history of events or for the characterisation of Achaemenid institutions we should rather be interested in him as a highly influential source for Greek views of the Orient'.
[15] Sherwin-White (1991), 71-86. Kosmin (2013), 204.

(albeit Egyptian not Babylonian) for a Greek audience.[16] Although there are numerous studies exploring the influence of Mesopotamian and Greek literature on Berossus' *Babyloniaka*, there is currently no scholarship comparing Berossus' text to imperial Greek literature.[17]

In this thesis I consider Berossus' *Babyloniaka* alongside Lucian's *De Dea Syria* and the *Kyranides,* exploring the methods of cultural transmission and the narrative devices they employ, which is then compared to Iamblichus' *Babyloniaka*. These texts are selected due to their non-Greek authorship and their appeal to Greek associations of Babylon/ Mesopotamia's with ancient lore, as each author presents themselves as transmitting esoteric knowledge. Whilst the *Kyranides* remains a largely neglected text, with M. Waegmann providing the only substantial study on the text, *De Dea Syria* has been subject to much research. The early scholarship on *De Dea Syria* focuses on the debate regarding the authorship of the text, but since Jane Lightfoot's comprehensive analysis, Lucian is generally-accepted as the author.[18] Subsequent and more recent scholarship on *De Dea Syria* tends to consider what the text reveals about Mesopotamian identity during the period, as the text provides the only contemporary account of polytheistic worship in the Roman Near East written by someone claiming to be an insider.[19] I continue this line of study though incorporating the ancient novels into the discussion.

Ancient novelists possessed a greater freedom and flexibility than historians, orators and philosophers, as they could entertain alternative realities and engage with marvels without the necessity of explaining or understanding them.[20] Hence, the two novels I focus on, Chariton's *Callirhoe* and Iamblichus' *Babyloniaka,* are able to appeal to the fantasies of their Greek audience: Chariton enters the seraglio (allowing his readers to view restricted zones),[21] whilst Iamblichus heavily emphasises the magic and wonder of Babylon. Although in recent years Iamblichus' *Babyloniaka* has received more scholarly attention, these studies predominantly

---

[16] Verbrugghe & Wickersham (2001); Moyer (2013); Dillery (2015).
[17] Drews (1975); Van der Spek (2008); Dalley (2013b); Kosmin (2013); Tuplin (2013); Haubold (2013a); Haubold (2013b).
[18] Lightfoot (2003).
[19] Kaizer (2016), 277.
[20] Stephens (2008), 70.
[21] See Llewellyn-Jones (2013b).

focus on Iamblichus himself, and his influences, or on the intertextuality between the *Babyloniaka* and other ancient novels.[22] Roger Beck, who discusses the possibly Mithraic allegories,[23] Helen Morales, who addresses the political implications of the text,[24] and most recently Catherine Connors and Dimitri Kasprzyk,[25] who both provide an eco-critical analysis of the novel, are exceptions to the general trend. This thesis considers what Iamblichus' novel tells us about Babylon in the Greek *imaginaire*, exploring the different narrative devices Iamblichus employed to appeal to the Greek fascination of Babylon depicting the city as a licentious, dangerous and wondrous space. I argue that no other text better embodies the multiple strands of the Greek imagination of Babylon than Iamblichus' novel.

Contribution to research

Although during the Hellenistic period Babylon declined into obscurity, the city remained vivid and alive in the Greek imagination well into the imperial period. Despite this, the presentation of Babylon in imperial Graeco-Roman literature remains relatively unexplored. This study seeks to fill this void, focusing predominantly on texts from the imperial period, including *De Dea Syria* and the *Kyranides*, and with a particular emphasis on the ancient novels of Chariton and Iamblichus.

To my knowledge, there are currently no studies providing a concise, systematic overview of the Greek presentation of Babylon in the literary imagination. Greek literature often conflated the terms 'Persians', 'Medes', 'Mages', 'Babylonians', 'Chaldaeans', 'Assyrians' and 'Syrians'.[26] Even the legendary Hanging Garden of Babylon was most likely located in the Assyrian capital of Nineveh (known temporarily as Old Babylon).[27] Hence, rather than focusing the Greeks presentation

---

[22] Danek (2000); Gärtner (2010); Dowden (2018); Kavanou (2019); Dowden (2019); Bowie (forth.).
[23] Beck (1982).
[24] Morales (2006).
[25] Connors (2017); Kasprzyk (2017).
[26] Ogden (2002), 33-51; Ogden (2008), 77-86. On the conflation of Assyria with Babylon see Dalley (1993), 7-12; Dalley (1994), 46-50; Dalley (2013a), 107-127 who accumulates substantial evidence of Greek literature conflating Babylon with Nineveh, which was confusingly known as 'Old Babylon'.
[27] Dalley (1993); Dalley (1994); Dalley (2013a) convincingly argues the Hanging Garden was located in Nineveh through the use of literary (Greek and cuneiform) and topographical evidence. Dalley (2013a), 45-6 compares the terrains of Southern Iraq (Babylon) to Norther Iraq (Assyria) concluding that the mountainous, hilly terrain of the latter was more suited to the Hanging Garden.

of a specific Mesopotamian culture, this thesis instead considers how certain behaviours and practices became associated with Babylon as a city.

This thesis provides a Greek-centric and literary perspective, considering the impact of Babylon in the Greek cultural imagination. Rather than debunking the veracity of the Greek depiction of Babylon, I instead explore how Babylon ignited different strands of the imagination, exploring how the city became: a favoured setting for romantic narratives, a space of scientific wonder, associated with magical practices and political intrigue, and presented as a transformative space which inverted gender boundaries and subverted expectations. This study considers different lenses through which the Greeks viewed Babylon, covering a wide range of sources spanning from fifth century BCE up until the third/fourth century CE,[28] which includes historiographies, biographies, magico-medical texts, comic dialogues, and (especially) the ancient novel.

Thesis outline

This thesis is split into three thematically-organised chapters. Although chapters one and two address Greek presentation of 'Mesopotamia', the emphasis remains on Babylon, and how certain practices and behaviours were initially associated, or belonged to, Mesopotamia but gradually became affiliated specifically to Babylon. The first two chapters also lay the groundwork for the final chapter, which discusses how the ancient novel incorporated the different strands of the Greek imagination of Babylon.

Chapter one explores the Greek presentation of Mesopotamian court-life, discussing the recurring literary types which were developed during the classical period, including scheming eunuchs, vengeful women and weak kings. The significance of Ctesias in establishing an image of femininity dominating in Babylon and how the royal hunt was employed as a barometer of effective kingship or evidence for the weakness and femininity of a ruler is discussed. The chapter also explores the Greek reception of Mesopotamian royal gardens, and how these gardens, especially the legendary Hanging Garden, became a source of wonder and

---

[28] The exact dating of the *Kyranides* is uncertain.

admiration in the Greek imagination. Sensationalised courts and the Hanging Garden continue to be associated with Babylon today, and the second chapter addresses the other aspect affiliated with Babylon: magic.

The second chapter focuses on esoteric wisdom and magical practices, specifically astrology and necromancy, which became affiliated with Babylon. The majority of the chapter explores the crossing of thresholds between Greece and Mesopotamia, discussing the methods of cultural transmission in three Greek texts with non-Greek authors: Berossus' *Babyloniaka,* Lucian's *De Dea Syria* and the *Kyranides.* These texts engaged with the magic and lore of the region, presenting themselves as transmitting a range of Mesopotamian knowledge. The authors each employ authenticating-devices to enhance their validity: Berossus draws upon ancient archives, Lucian presents himself as an initiate and the *Kyranides* combines pseudo-documentarism with the discovery of an iron stele, alongside the presence of a wandering wise-man, relying on the translation of a prisoner of war. These texts reaffirm Greek preconceptions of Mesopotamia as a wondrous space, whilst also hinting at the complexities of cultural identity and the political instability under imperialist rule, similar to Iamblichus' *Babyloniaka.*

The final chapter predominantly focuses on two ancient novels: Chariton's *Callirhoe* and Iamblichus' *Babyloniaka.* Babylon in the novelistic tradition was depicted as a highly-eroticised, dangerous and unstable space. This chapter demonstrates how Babylon was at the centre of the development of the Greek romantic imagination and how the ancient novel embodies the different strands of the Greek imagination, presenting the exoticism of the political and natural world alongside the esotericism and magical reputation of Babylon. I argue that Babylon was a liminal space in Greek literature, where the boundaries between history and fiction became distorted, socio-cultural boundaries were fragile, expectations subverted and nothing is really quite as it seems.

CHAPTER ONE

Greek Impressions of Mesopotamia: Sensationalised Courts and Wondrous Gardens

The genre of *Persica* emerged during the fifth and fourth centuries BCE, coinciding with the Graeco-Persian wars. *Persica* focused on the history and culture of the Persian Empire. Known authors of *Persica* include: Herodotus, Ctesias, Dionysius of Miletus, Charon of Lampsacus, Hellanicus of Lesbos, Dinon of Colophon and Heracleides of Cumae. The majority of these authors were from Asia Minor, some residing in cities under the intermittent control of the Achaemenids.[1] These authors attempted to understand their eastern neighbours (and occasional rulers), but also sought to establish a Greek identity distinct from the 'Other'.[2] Although recent scholarship argues that the Classical Greek reception of the Achaemenid Empire is more nuanced than previously credited,[3] clichés were nevertheless established during the period which cast the Persians as the 'Other' and laid the foundations of 'Orientalism'.[4]

Although Greek authors focussed predominantly on the empire of the Achaemenids specifically, owing to a certain vagueness in the Greek mind about the different cultures of Mesopotamia, stereotypes developed about people of the region more generally. The first half of this chapter focuses on three types that emerge from Greek literary representations of Mesopotamian courts: scheming eunuchs, vengeful women and weak kings. The purpose is to lay the groundwork for later chapters, where I will explore these types in the fictional literature of the imperial period, since depictions of Babylon at this later period are also entangled with receptions of the literature of the Classical past. Herodotus and Ctesias are both crucial figures in the Classical period who established and solidified numerous orientalist clichés associated with Mesopotamia in the Greek literary tradition. Ctesias of Cnidus was a

---

[1] Llewellyn-Jones & Robson (2010), 55.

[2] Sancisi-Weerdenburg (1987b); Hall (1989); Llewellyn-Jones and Robson (2010), 55. See Morgan (2016), 126-129 for an overview on scholarship addressing the Greek invention of the 'Other'.

[3] Gruen (2011); Morgan (2016).

[4] Saïd (1978), 56 in his seminal study regards Aeschylus as the first proponent of Orientalism. Cf. Sancisi-Weerdenburg (1987a) who considers Ctesias responsible for establishing numerous orientalist clichés.

physician at the court of Artaxerxes II (ruled ca. 405-359), and was the first Greek to write about Persia from the inside.[5] Female authority dominates in Ctesias' depictions of court life: eunuchs and women are at the centre of court intrigue, and Babylon is a space where traditional gender boundaries are transgressed. Ctesias' feminisation of Mesopotamia powerfully influenced the Greek imagination and subsequent accounts of Persia by Athenian writers during the fourth century BCE, including Plato and Isocrates, who similarly presented an image of a decadent and declining Persian Empire.

The second half of this chapter moves away from the world of court-intrigue into the royal gardens and the royal hunt, exploring their ideological importance in the Persian empire, and their impact on the Greek cultural imagination. The current research on Mesopotamian royal gardens tends to focus on the functions of these gardens or on unravelling the mysteries surrounding the precise nature or location of the Hanging Garden of Babylon. Whilst this chapter does allude to ambiguities surrounding the Hanging Garden, mainly its irrigation system, the primary focus is assessing the Greek reception of Mesopotamian royal gardens. Greeks travelling through Mesopotamia during the fifth and fourth centuries BCE encountered Persian-designed royal gardens.[6] These luxurious, grand gardens were a contrast to the small, kitchen-gardens Greeks were accustomed to. The first section demonstrates how Greeks were aware of the ideological importance of gardens and the hunt, and used the royal hunt as a barometer of effective kingship, a feature the ancient novelists similarly employed. The second section discusses the Greek admiration for Persian hunting-parks and *paradeisoi*. I show how this influenced their very language, through their adoption of the term *paradeisos* into Greek, and influenced their own garden-design as well. The third section explores the marvellous Hanging Garden specifically, and investigates why it continued to be considered a marvel even after Greek technology surpassed its technology. The final section explores how the rise of ancient romances opened up a whole new fascination with Babylon and added new strands to the reception of Mesopotamian royal gardens, which became the setting for romantic and sexual endeavours.

---

[5] Llewellyn-Jones & Robson (2010), 52.
[6] Greeks mistakenly considered the contents and purposes of these royal gardens to be an unique Persian royal institution. See Canepa (2018), 350.

Sensationalised Courts

a) Scheming Eunuchs

Among the characteristic features of Ctesias' *Persica* is the omnipresence of eunuchs at the Achaemenid court.[7] Although eunuchs were also a feature of Assyrian and Median courts, Ctesias depicts them at their most influential during the Persian Empire. In contrast to popular belief, eunuchs were far more likely to be found in the company of the king than in the presence of women.[8] Indeed, every Achaemenid king in Ctesias is flanked by at least one eunuch.[9] These eunuchs acted predominantly as advisors to the king, occasionally as military commanders (§10; §31),[10] and as agents entrusted to transport the king's corpse (§9; §23; §47).[11]

Ctesias presents eunuchs at the centre of court intrigue and willing to betray their masters. The loyalty of Izabates, who denounced the conspiracy of the Magus and was consequently executed by the usurpers (§15), and Bagapates, who watched over Darius' tomb for seven years (§23), are exceptions.[12] Eunuchs assisted in the successful assassinations of the Magus (§16),[13] Xerxes I (§33)[14] and Xerxes II (§48).[15] Eunuchs were also complicit in a number of failed coups against members of the royal household, including the Assyrian Queen Semiramis (20.1)[16], the Median King Astyages (§6),[17] and the Persian kings Artaxerxes I (§34),[18] and Darius II (§54).[19]

---

[7] Lenfant (2012), 258.

[8] Tougher (2008), 13; Lenfant (2012), 269-272.

[9] Briant (2002a), 268.

[10] F 13 = Photius, *Bib* 72 p. 37a26-40a5 (§9-33). All testimonia and fragments on Ctesias follow the numbering of Llewellyn-Jones & Robson (2010), 91-219.

[11] F 13; F15 = Photius, *Bib* 72 p. 41b38-43b2 (§47-56).

[12] F 13. However, Bagapates had conspired with the Seven in the overthrow of the Magus, before establishing himself as a loyal servant of Darius (§16).

[13] F 13. Bagapates led the Seven to the Magus' chamber.

[14] F 13. The powerful courtier Artapanus conspired with the eunuch Spamitres to kill Xerxes and frame his son Darius. Cf. F 13a = Athenaeus, 13.10 p. 560de, where Xerxes' throat is cut by his son.

[15] F 15. Secyndianus, the illegitimate son of Artaxerxes I, recruited the help of the eunuch Pharnacyas to assassinate Xerxes II, Artaxerxes' legitimate son.

[16] F 1b = Diodorus, 2.1.4-28.7. Semiramis discovers the plot and willingly abdicates the throne. Cf. F 1g = Eusebius, *Chronography,* p.29, 3-10 Karst, where Semiramis is killed by her son Ninus.

[17] F 9 = Photius, *Bib* p. 36a9 – 37a25 (§1-8). See also F 9a = Tzetzes, *Chiliades,* 1.90-103 [Kiessling 87-100].

[18] F 14 = Photius, p. 40a5-41b37 (§34-46).

[19] F 15.

Artoxares exemplifies the scheming and ambitious nature of eunuchs in Ctesias.[20] After participating in the conspiracy against Secyndianus (§50), Artoxares established himself as a trusted advisor to the new king Darius II (§51). However, Artoxares' loyalty was only temporary, and he proceeded to conspire against Darius (§54). Artoxares was not simply complicit in a plot to assassinate Darius; he actually instigated the conspiracy himself, owing to his aspiration to kingship. However, he was hindered by his effeminate appearance, and enlisted the help of a woman to acquire a fake beard and moustache. This woman betrayed him, and he was handed over to Darius' wife, Queen Parysatis, for punishment. This episode illustrates the marked and unusual predominance of non-male power in the Persian court (Greeks did not consider eunuchs to be men),[21] and reiterates the role of eunuchs as kingmakers. The stability of the king's court relies on the support of eunuchs and women.

Ctesias' depiction of scheming eunuchs contrasts starkly with the image of the 'faithful eunuch' presented in Herodotus. Eunuchs played a less influential role in Herodotus and are only alluded to on ten occasions.[22] Where they are mentioned, eunuchs are depicted as trusted servants to the king, acting as bodyguards, spies, messengers, and even guardians to the king's sons.[23] Eunuchs are even prepared to die for the master, as demonstrated by the Magus' eunuchs' attempt to block the Seven's entry to the royal bedchamber.[24] Herodotus is not the only Classical Greek source to portray eunuchs in such a way. Xenophon's *Cyropaedia* similarly presents eunuchs as trustworthy and courageous servants.[25] Cyrus entrusts matters of security to eunuchs, including acting as bodyguards and messengers to Panthea.[26] After Panthea commits suicide, her eunuchs proceed to kill themselves out of grief, demonstrating the extent of their loyalty and courage.[27]

---

[20] F 15.

[21] Aristotle *Gen.an.* 5.3.783b-784a identified eunuchs with women. See Lenfant (2012), 275-6, fn. 101, 102.

[22] Herodotus 1.117; 3.4; 3.48-49; 3.77-78; 3.92; 3.130; 4.43; 6.9; 6.32; 7.187; 8.104-105.

[23] In Herodotus 8.104 Xerxes entrusts the eunuch Harmotimus to guard his sons.

[24] Herodotus 3.77.

[25] Xen *Cyr.* 6.1.33-4; 7.3.3; 7.4.14-5; 7.5.60-5.

[26] Xen *Cyr.* 7.5.60-65 Cyrus trusts loyalty of eunuchs as they had no family ties. See also, Briant (2002a), 270-272.

[27] Xen *Cyr.* 7.4.14-5.

In contrast to Ctesias, eunuchs in Herodotus and Xenophon never seek to manipulate courtly affairs nor conspire against the king. The differing depictions suggest there was a certain ambivalence concerning eunuchs' status and the Greek attitude towards them during the Classical period. But it also suggests that the portrayal of eunuchs depended on the lens through which Persia was observed. Xenophon's *Cyropaedia* was a work of Greek political theory,[28] and whilst Herodotus focused on Graeco-Persian relations, neither author delves much into the intricacies of the Achaemenid court. In contrast, Ctesias provides a glimpse into the court in which he resided and throughout his narrative he engages with tales of intrigue, feeding the Greek fascination with the east by placing eunuchs at the centre of plots.

Whereas authors of earlier *Persica,* such as Herodotus, tended to focus on the history and culture of Persia, subsequent authors focused on court intrigue and gossip.[29] Like Ctesias, these later *Persica* (the sources of the last chapters of Plutarch's *Artaxerxes*) as well as the histories of Alexander, present eunuchs as the personal attendants of the king and influential figures of the court,[30] either participating in,[31] or denouncing court plots.[32] Eunuchs also began to appear in new sexual roles such as lovers of the king. The eunuch Tiridates was loved by Artaxerxes II,[33] and Bagoas was the lover of Darius III and Alexander.[34] The most influential figure was Bagoas (not the aforementioned), the powerful eunuch from the last decade of the Achaemenid Empire. Bagoas held many important official functions, owned considerable property,[35] and was regularly depicted as a wicked kingmaker. He managed to assassinate king Artaxerxes III and his heir, Artaxerxes IV, before securing the throne for Darius III. Reinhard Pirngruber considers Bagoas to be an amplification of the clichés that have their roots in Ctesias's *Persica.*[36] There are certainly similarities between Ctesias' Artoxares and Bagoas: both

---

[28] Lenfant (2012), 273.

[29] Brosius (1996), 105; Morgan (2016), 190.

[30] Dinon, *BNJ FGrHist 690* F 12a = Athenaeus, *Deipnosophistae,* 14.67.652 bc; Herakleides of Cyme, *BNJ FGrHist 689* F 2 = = Athenaeus, *Deipnosophistae,* 4.26 p.145a-146a; Plutarch, *Art.* 12; 30.

[31] Curtius 6.4.10-12; Plutarch, *Art.* 15; Diodorus 11.69.1; 17.5.3-6.

[32] Plutarch, *Art.* 29 where a eunuch denounces a plot against King Artaxerxes II. See Lenfant (2012), 273-4.

[33] Aelian, *HM.* 12.1

[34] Curtius 6.5.22-3.

[35] Bagoas important official functions included: military command, administration of satrapies and the function of chiliarch. He also owned gardens in Babylon and a palace in Susa.

[36] Pirngruber (2011), 283-4.

eunuchs secured the ascension of a king and established themselves as loyal servants, before being killed for conspiring against the king.[37] Bagoas helped entrench the notion of eunuchs at the centre of palace intrigue, and became a character in Near Eastern romances.[38] According to Pliny, Bagoas was the Persian word for a eunuch, demonstrating the extent Bagoas became solidified in Greek imagination as *the* caricature of the scheming eunuch.[39]

As Shaun Tougher points out, then, "Eunuchs could be presented as utterly treacherous as well as utterly loyal".[40] Texts that focussed on Graeco-Persian relations tended to depict eunuchs as loyal servants, with little influence over political affairs. Conversely, texts that concentrated on the inner workings of the court presented eunuchs as scheming in nature and at the centre of court intrigue. Ctesias' portrayal of eunuchs as active and influential agents within the court, rather than the trustworthy background characters of Herodotus and Xenophon, came to dominate the Greek imagination, as demonstrated by the prominence of Bagoas and the increasingly court-centric focus of subsequent *Persica*, and it was this image of the scheming eunuch which influenced the ancient novelists.

b) Vengeful Women

Herodotus and Ctesias were also fundamental in shaping ideas about Mesopotamian women in the Greek imagination. Both authors depict women influencing the political landscape of Mesopotamia, either as autonomous warrior-queens or working within the court structure and manipulating the king's judgement. Warrior women were objects of fascination and even admiration amongst Greek audiences.[41] Herodotus' and Ctesias' warrior-queens possess a number of admirable but distinctly masculine characteristics. Herodotus praises the 'manly courage' of Artemisia of Halicarnassus,[42] whilst Ctesias' Semiramis and Zarinea of Saces both found cities and demonstrate courage in war, leading multiple military

---

[37] On Bagoas, see Diodorus 17.5.3-6. See also Briant (2002a), 269-270; Lenfant (2012), 274.
[38] Aelian, *HM* 6.8; *Judith Romance* 12.11. See Briant (2002a), 270.
[39] Pliny, *NH* 13.9.41
[40] Tougher (2008), 96.
[41] Romm (1998), 170-171.
[42] Herodotus 7.99.

expeditions.[43] Autonomous warrior-queens were praised for their masculine virtues, but they also committed acts of excessive violence, as is the case with Herodotus' Tomyris of Massagetae and Pheretime.

Tomyris inflicts on Cyrus the only defeat of his reign, but her most memorable deed is in the aftermath of victory, where she brutally decapitates Cyrus' corpse and plunges his head into a skin filled with blood.[44] Tomyris did this in retribution for her son, who was killed in a prior battle against Cyrus. A precedent of bodily-mutilation committed in retaliation and vengeance is found in Homer.[45] However, such acts were always inflicted by highly-ranked men in extreme anger.[46] In contrast, Herodotus presents women as capable of committing such deeds, including the mutilation of other living women.[47] Pheretime, like Tomyris, seeks to avenge her son, and after capturing the city of Baca she proceeds to crucify all the men and cut off the breasts of their women.[48] Interestingly, Pheretime was of Dorian ethnicity, suggesting Herodotus considered anyone experiencing extreme grief; whether male or female, Greek or non-Greek, could inflict such cruelties. However, cruelty and vengeance became particularly associated with royal women of the Achaemenid court.

Women were a prominent feature of the Achaemenid court: Achaemenid kings were polygamous and maintained many concubines.[49] Kings maintained numerous women in their court as a manifestation of their virility, wealth and control over the land,[50] but most importantly to produce many children.[51] Concubines tended to be foreign and acquired through gift exchange, tribute or war booty, whereas the king's wives tended to be Persian and on that basis considered superior to the

---

[43] Courage, independence and intelligence were all considered masculine characteristics. See Penrose (2016), 23-27.

[44] Herodotus 1.214.

[45] For bodily-mutilation in Homer, see Kucewicz (2016).

[46] Most famously, Achilles' prolonged mutilation of Hector's corpse in retaliation over Patrocles' death. Homer, *Il.* 22.369-75; 22.395-404; 23.21; 24.14-18; 24.416-17. See Kucewicz (2016), 432-435 for a discussion on Achilles' maltreatment of Hector's corpse.

[47] Hazewindus (2004), 92-3.

[48] Herodotus 4.202.

[49] The number of Persian concubines was usually listed as three hundred and sixty: Herakleides *FGrH BNJ 689* F1 = Athenaeus, *Deipnosophistae* 12.8 p.514 BC; Plutarch *Art.* 27.2. Cf. Curtius 6.6.8 lists number as three hundred and sixty-five.

[50] Llewellyn-Jones (2013a) 119.

[51] Strabo 15.3.17 'For the sake of having many children'.

concubines. Dinon provides an insight into the hierarchy amongst women of the court:[52]

> παρὰ δὲ Πέρσαις ἀνέχεται ἡ βασίλεια τοῦ πλήθους τῶν παλλακίδων διὰ τὸ ὡς δεσπότην ἄρχειν τῆς γαμετῆς τὸν βασιλέα, ἔτι δὲ καὶ διὰ τὸ τὴν βασιλίδα, ὥς φησιν Δίνων ἐν τοῖς Περσικοῖς, ὑπὸ τῶν παλλακίδων θρησκεύεσθαι· προσκυνοῦσι γοῦν αὐτήν.

> Among the Persians, the queen bears with patience the fact that (the king has) many concubines, because the king rules his lawful wife like her master; and moreover because of the fact that the queen, as Dinon says in his *Persika,* is venerated by the concubines: certainly, they prostrate themselves before her. [trans. E. Almagor (2018)].

Whether there was a hierarchy amongst the wives is less certain. Dinon refers to the king's wife in the singular, and it was typical of Greek sources to only name one wife of the king. This perhaps suggests there was a 'chief' wife for each king, although there is no official Persian title to support this claim.[53] The presence of numerous women certainly led to power struggles within the court, as women attempted to consolidate their status and secure inheritance for their favoured sons.[54]

However, in contrast to scheming eunuchs, Greek sources never present Achaemenid women as conspiring to treason. Instead, royal women worked within the boundaries of the court system as they sought to exert their influence over the king and persuade his judgement.[55] When it came to inflicting cruel punishments on their enemies, Achaemenid women would patiently await the right circumstances to approach the king to gain his consent. Usually, Achaemenid women severely punished those who had harmed their family or those who threatened their status and authority.

Herodotus' depiction of Amestris, wife of Xerxes I, demonstrates the extent royal women were willing to go to protect their bloodline. When Xerxes offers his

---

[52] Dinon *BNJ FGrH 690* F27 = Athenaeus, *Deipnosophistae* 13.556B.
[53] Llewellyn-Jones (2013a), 114 suggests this may reflect the monogamous Greeks' inability to contemplate the polygamous nature of Achaemenid kings.
[54] Llewellyn-Jones (2013a),120.
[55] Brosius (1996), 120; Llewellyn-Jones (2013a), 111.

lover Artanyte anything she desires, Artanyte requests the shawl which Amestris had gifted Xerxes. Although Xerxes urges Artanyte to reconsider, even offering her cities and an army instead, Araynte insists and Xerxes relents, giving her the shawl.[56] When Amestris finds out, she plots her revenge, though not against Artanyte, but against Artanyte's mother, the wife of Masistes and sister-in-law to Xerxes. Amestris waits until Xerxes' birthday, whereupon the king holds a banquet and distributes gifts, in the knowledge that Xerxes could not refuse her request for Masistes' wife.[57]

The royal robe was a symbol of legitimate kingship, and therefore in demanding the shawl, Artanyte was claiming sovereignty for her family.[58] Hence Amestris' decision to punish Artanyte's mother, who was her equal on dynastic terms, rather than Artanyte herself. It also explains the manner of punishment: Amestris brutally mutilates Masistes' wife, first cutting off her breasts and feeding them to the dogs, then cutting off nose, ears, lips, and tongue, before sending the disfigured woman back home.[59] During the Achaemenid Empire, mutilated individuals could not become sovereign, and it was a common practice for Achaemenid kings to mutilate treasonous individuals. Therefore, Amestris halts Masistes' family ambitions and does so in an emblematic way: by removing his wife's breasts symbolising her motherhood and dynastic fecundity.[60] Amestris' mutilation of Masistes' wife was not simply a sadistic and irrational act, but rather a method to assert her own sovereignty and her son's position as heir.

Ctesias expands upon the precedent established by Herodotus, and offers numerous instances of royal women devising gruesome and innovative executions for their enemies.[61] Unlike Herodotus' Amestris, who acts to protect her family from harm, Ctesias' Amestris seeks vengeance on family members who have already suffered. On the first occasion, Amestris seeks vengeance for her son Achaemenides, who was killed by the Libyan rebel Inarus (§36).[62] King Artaxerxes I

---

[56] Herodotus 9.109.
[57] Herodotus 9.110-111.
[58] Sancisi-Weerdenburg (1983), 20-34; Llewellyn-Jones (2013a), 138.
[59] Herodotus 9.112.
[60] Llewellyn-Jones (2013a), 138.
[61] For example, F 9 (§6) Amytis the Elder, the wife of Cyrus the Great, blinded, flayed alive and crucified the eunuch Petesacas.
[62] F14 = Photius, *Bib* p. 40a5 – 41b37 (§34-46).

initially grants Inarus, and the Greek mercenaries who aided him, amnesty for killing his brother. However, Amestris for five years continually asks Artaxerxes for permission to punish Inarus, and the persistence pays off, as Artaxerxes grants his mother's wish. Amestris proceeds to impale Inarus and behead fifty Greeks. The number of people Amestris executes is staggering considering the king's initial reluctance to hand over a single Greek. The episode shows the determination of royal women to fulfil their vendettas but it also reiterates how royal women would await the king's consent before acting, even if it took five years to acquire. Amestris faces less resistance when she seeks to punish the physician Apollonides of Cos, who had tricked her daughter, Amytis, into sexual relations (§44). This time Artaxerxes quickly grants Amestris' request and hands Apollonides over to her. Amestis proceeds to punish Apollonides for two months and then buries him alive. The final instance where Amestris seeks vengeance concerns the death of her grandson Zopyrus, where she has the man responsible crucified (§45).

Ctesias' depiction of Amestris presents her as calculated, persistent and capable of inflicting cruelty on multiple occasions and in numerous gruesome ways. But he also presents another, more diplomatic side to her character. Ctesias describes Amestris as an advisor to the king (§42) and shows her successfully interceding on behalf of the satrap Megabyzus, saving his life in the process (§43).[63] Indeed, throughout his *Persica,* Ctesias presents royal women as acting as advisors to the king, occasionally managing to influence the king's judgement. This is especially true of Parysatis, the central female figure in Ctesias.

Of all royal women, Parysatis intervenes the most frequently in politics. Her husband, Darius II, relies predominantly on Parysatis' advice (§50), despite having three eunuchs in his entourage whom he could call upon.[64] The extent of Parysatis' influence is demonstrated when she proceeds to punish Aristes, the rebellious brother of Darius, despite Darius' hesitation and reluctance (§52).[65] Following Darius' death and the accession of their son Artaxerxes II, Parysatis competed with Stateria,

---

[63] Amestris interceded on Megabyszus' behalf alongside her daughter Amytis and the eunuch Artoxares.
[64] F 15.
[65] F 15.

the wife of Artaxerxes II, for influence over the king. Parysatis seeks revenge on everyone involved in the death of Cyrus the Younger, her favourite son.[66] Ctesias describes multiple instances in which Parysatis manipulates Artaxerxes into punishing (often horrifically) those involved in Cyrus' death.[67] Parysatis gradually achieves her vengeance and is involved in the deaths of a Carian (§14) Mithridates (§15-16), and finally the eunuch Masabates (§17), who had mutilated Cyrus' corpse.[68] In a similar manner to Herodotus' Amestris, Parysatis patiently waits for the right moment before tricking Artaxerxes into handing Masabates over to her.[69]

> λαβοῦσα δή ποτε τὸν Ἀρταξέρξην ὡρμημένον ἀλύειν σχολῆς οὔσης,
> προύκαλεῖτο περὶ χιλίων δαρεικῶν κυβεῦσαι· καὶ κυβεύοντα
> περιεῖδε νικῆσαι καὶ τὸ χρυσίον ἀπέδωκε. Προσποιουμένη
> δ' ἀνιᾶσθαι καὶ φιλονικεῖν, ἐκέλευσεν αὖθις ἐξ ἀρχῆς περὶ
> εὐνούχου διακυβεῦσαι, κἀκεῖνος ὑπήκουσε.

> [17.5] One day Parysatis, catching Artaxerxes with nothing to do and beginning to roam idly about, challenged him to a game of dice with a stake of 1,000 darics. And she saw to it that he won at the game and she handed over the gold. Pretending that she was annoyed and keen to get her own back, she suggested another game, the stake this time being a eunuch. And the king consented. [trans. Llewellyn-Jones & Robson (2010)].

Parysatis proceeds to win the game and claims the eunuch Masabates as her prize. Once in her possession, Parysatis flays him alive, impales his body on a stake and pegs out his stretched-out skin.[70] When Artaxerxes discovers Parysatis' deception, he reproaches her:

> γενομένων δὲ τούτων, καὶ βασιλέως χαλεπῶς φέροντος καὶ
> παροξυνομένου πρὸς αὐτήν, εἰρωνευομένη μετὰ γέλωτος, ὡς ἡδύς
> "ἔφασκεν, εἰ καὶ μακάριος, εἰ χαλεπαίνεις διὰ γέροντα πονηρὸν
> εὐνοῦχον ἐγὼ δὲ χιλίους ἐκκυβευθεῖσα δαρεικοὺς σιωπῶ καὶ στέργω."
> βασιλεὺς μὲν οὖν ἐφ' οἷς ἐξηπατήθη μεταμελόμενος ἡσυχίαν ἦγεν,
> ἡ δὲ Στάτειρα καὶ πρὸς τἆλλα φανερῶς ἠναντιοῦτο, καὶ τούτοις
> ἐδυσχέραινεν, ὡς ἄνδρας εὐνοϊκοὺς καὶ πιστοὺς βασιλεῖ διὰ Κῦρον
> ὠμῶς καὶ παρανόμως ἀπολλυούσης αὐτῆς.

---

[66] F 17 = Plutarch, *Art.* 2.3-3.6.
[67] F 26 = Plutarch, *Art.* 14-17.
[68] F 26.
[69] F 26.
[70] Cf. F 16 = Photius, *Bib* p.43b3-44a19 (§57-67). In Photius' account, the eunuch Bagapates cuts off the head of Cyrus' body. Photius proceeds to recall a similar story, in which Parysatis plays dice with Artaxerxes, claims Bagapates as her prize, then flays him alive and crucifies him.

[17.8] When this was done, the King found it intolerable and was angry with her, but she feigned ignorance and with a smile said, 'How sweet you are! Happy for you that you get angry on account of a useless old eunuch! I, on the other hand, lost 1000 darics at dice, and have accepted my loss and not said a word'. [9] And so the King, although he regretted being deceived like this, held his tongue. But Stateira openly opposed her in other matters and was particularly disapproving of the fact that, because of Cyrus, she was brutally and lawlessly killing eunuchs and other men who were loyal to the King. [trans. Llewellyn-Jones & Robson (2010)].

Parysatis maintains control of the situation and avoids punishment from Artaxerxes. Whilst Artaxerxes reluctantly accepts the situation, his wife Stateira openly opposes Parysatis, and the two women compete for influence over the court. Stateira persuades Artaxerxes to execute the Spartan Clearchus, an ally of Parysatis (§69).[71] The factional infighting between the women ends after Parysatis resorts to poisoning Stateira.[72] Until this point, Parysatis had managed to accomplish her personal vendettas by remaining within the limits of permissible court conduct, but by poisoning Stateira, she acted without the king's permission. Parysatis is consequently punished and exiled to Babylon.

One would expect Parysatis to be exiled to a city far removed from the political sphere, but Babylon, as one of the capitals of the Achaemenid Empire, remained a politically and administratively important city. The 'Babylonisation' of the Achaemenid royal line after Artaxerxes I demonstrates Babylon's influence in Achaemenid affairs. Artaxerxes I had numerous children with Babylonian women, including Parysatis and the future kings Secyndianus and Ochus (Darius II).[73] Parysatis proceeded to marry her half-brother Darius II, making their children (including Artaxerxes II) half-Babylonian. Thus, Parysatis' exile to Babylon was closer to a homecoming than punishment. It was more a symbolic gesture on Artaxerxes' II part: a futile attempt to present himself as maintaining some authority over his mother. In reality, irreversible damage had already been done. Parysatis' actions undermined the king's authority and exposed Artaxerxes as lacking control. Loyalty to the king does not guarantee protection, as the fate of the eunuch Masabates shows, and Artaxerxes cannot even protect his own wife owing to his

---

[71] F 27 = Photius, *Bib* p. 44a20 – b19 (§68-71); F28 = Plutarch, *Art.* 18.
[72] F 27 (§70); F 29b = Plutarch, *Art.* 19; T 15b Plutarch, *Art.* 18.6-7.
[73] F 15.

inability to control his own mother's violent inclinations. Instead, power and control in Artaxerxes' court resides with Parysatis. This is just one instance in Ctesias where female authority prevails over the Persian court, and in this particular case, it is a Babylonian woman, presenting Babylon as influencing Achaemenid affairs and continuing to play an important role in shaping the political landscape of Mesopotamia.

c) *Weak Kings*

The influence of women and eunuchs in Ctesias contributed towards the image of weak kings.[74] Although eunuchs play a less influential role in Herodotus, women are shown to influence the political landscape. Herodotus even applies the appellation 'all-powerful' to Atossa,[75] the wife of Darius and mother of Xerxes, and presents her as persuading Darius to invade Greece.[76] In doing this, Herodotus entirely omits the political background of Darius' Greece campaign and instead presents it as the result of a woman's influence. We have already seen how Ctesias' Parysatis subverted Artaxerxes' authority by poisoning his wife, but even when royal Achaemenid women worked within the confines of the court, their actions threatened to destabilised the Empire. In Herodotus, Amestris' mutilation of Masistes' wife prompted Masistes to rebel,[77] whilst in Ctesias, Amestris' execution of Inarus and fifty Greeks led to Megabyzus rebelling (§40-2).[78] Where women exerted their influence, the king's control and sovereignty was threatened.

The image of a decadent Persia, where kings were idle and isolated themselves surrounded with the luxury of the palace, often in the sole company of women and eunuchs, became increasingly common during the fourth century BCE.[79] In Herodotus, luxury plays an inconsistent role in the fortune of the Persian Empire.[80] Cyrus the Great is able to defeat the Medes and Lydians because Persia is comparatively tough, rigorous and severe, but Cyrus fails to defeat the Massagetae,

---

[74] Hall (1989), 157; Brosius (1996), 122; Lenfant (2012), 275-6.
[75] Herodotus 7.3.
[76] Herodotus 3.134.
[77] Although it is Xerxes' uncontrolled licentiousness which prompts Amestris' mutilation of Masistes' wife, and therefore blame for the subsequent rebellion also rests with Xerxes.
[78] F14.
[79] For the Greek depiction of decadence in the Persian Empire see Briant (2002b); Abe (2016).
[80] Gruen (2011), 27.

led by Tomyris, because they are the 'harder' people. Rather than Herodotus, the tradition of Persian decadence is more clearly rooted in Ctesias' work.

Powerful women are pervasive in Ctesias' Babylon. Ctesias provides the first Greek account of Semiramis' foundation of Babylon.[81] Not only was Ctesias' Babylon founded by a woman, it was the site of exile for Parysatis, the most influential Achaemenid royal woman.[82] Ctesias also depicts Babylon as a place where gender boundaries become disorientated, by presenting numerous male rulers of Babylon as effeminate. In Babylon, kings and rulers were suspectable to more than the persuasions of women, and ended up embodying feminine characteristics themselves, in both their appearance and mannerisms. The Assyrian kings Ninyas and Sardanapalus both indulged in idle luxury, did not hunt, and spent their time within the palace walls surrounded by women and eunuchs.[83] Sardanapalus' shaved beard and smoothed skin even resembled the physical appearance of a eunuch.[84] This effeminate behaviour continues during the Median Empire, when Nanarus, the king's representative in Babylon, dressed like a woman. The tale of Nanarus and Parsondes particularly highlights the dominance of femininity and the potentially transformative effects of Babylon.[85]

> ...ἦν ἐν Μήδοις τότε κατά τε ἀνδρείαν καὶ ῥώμην δοκιμώτατος Παρσώνδης, παρά τε βασιλεῖ μάλιστα ἐπαινούμενος καὶ ἐν Πέρσαις, ὅθεν ἦν γένος, ἐπί τε εὐβουλίαι καὶ κάλλει σώματος, δεινός τε καὶ θῆρας αἱρεῖν ἐν σταδίαι τε μάχηι καὶ ἀπὸ ἅρματος καὶ ἵππου μάχεσθαι. Οὗτος ὁρῶν Νάναρον τὸν Βαβυλώνιον διαπρεπεῖ κόσμωι χρώμενον ἀμφὶ τὸ σῶμα καὶ ἐλλόβια ἔχοντα καὶ κατεξυρημένον εὖ μάλα, γυναικώδη τε καὶ ἄναλκιν, ἔπειθεν Ἀρταῖον ἀφελέσθαι αὐτὸν τὴν ἀρχὴν καὶ ἑαυτῶι δοῦναι, δυσχεραίνων σφόδρα τὸν ἄνθρωπον.

> [1] ... there was at that time amongst the Medes a man called Parsondes who was held in particularly high regard for his bravery and strength.[86] Because of his wise counsel and physical beauty he was the object of much praise both in court and among the Persian – he was Persian by birth – and was talented

---

[81] Although according Haubold (2013b), 107 parts of the legend appear older than Ctesias.

[82] Babylonian records (Murašu) show that Parysatis owned considerable estates in the region. See Llewellyn-Jones (2013a), 112.

[83] F 1b (§21, §23); F 1n = Athenaeus, 12.38 p. 528ef; F 1oa = Eusebius, *Chronography* p. 29, 10–26 Karst; F 1pb = Aristotle, *Politics* 5.10.22 p. 1311b40–1312a4.

[84] F 1pa = Athenaeus, 12.38 p. 528f–529a.

[85] F 6b* = Nicolas of Damscus (Konstantinos VII Porphyrogennetos, *Exc. De Virtubus,* vol. 1 p.330.5 Büttner-Wobst = *BNJ FGrH 90* F4).

[86] Cf. F 5.

both at capturing wild beasts and at fighting, whether in hand-to-hand combat, from a chariot, or from horseback. When Parsondes saw Nanarus the Babylonian who clothed his body in eye-catching finery, wore earrings, and was particularly neatly shaven – womanish and feeble[87] – he tried to persuade Artaeus [Median king] to take Nanarus' territory away and give it to him instead: so much did he disapprove of the man. [trans. Llewellyn-Jones & Robson (2010)].

Nanarus, upon learning of Parsondes' complaints, offers a reward for his capture. A group of men trick Parsondes and take him to Babylon, where Nanarus punishes him by effeminizing him. He orders a eunuch to:

… ἄπαγε καὶ ξυρήσας τὸ ὅλον σῶμα καὶ κισηρίσας πλὴν κεφαλῆς δὶς τῆς ἡμέρας λοῦε καὶ σμῆχε ἀπὸ λεκίθου καὶ τοὺς ὀφθαλμοὺς ὑπογραφέσθω καὶ τὰς κόμας ἐμπλεκέσθω, ὥσπερ αἱ γυναῖκες· μανθανέτω δὲ ἄιδειν καὶ κιθαρίζειν καὶ ψάλλειν, ἵνα μοι μετὰ τῶν μουσουργῶν λειτουργῆι γυναικὶ ὡμοιωμένος, μεθ' ὧν καὶ δίαιταν ἕξει λεῖος ὢν τὸ σῶμα καὶ τὴν ἐσθῆτα τὴν αὐτὴν καὶ τὴν τέχνην ἔχων.

[3] … 'Take this man [Parsondes] away and shave and rub with pumice stone his whole body except his head. Wash him twice a day and soap him with egg yolk. Get him to paint underneath his eyes and to braid his hair, like women do. Make him learn to sing and play the cithara and the lyre so that, having become like a woman, he can do me service along with the other girl singers, whose way of life he will share, since his body will be smooth and he will possess the same clothing and skills'. [trans. Llewellyn-Jones & Robson (2010)].

Parsondes lived this way amongst the women for seven years. When King Artaeus learns of Parsondes' whereabouts, he sends an ambassador to Babylon to retrieve him. During the evening's entertainment, the ambassador is shocked to discover that the woman he considers most outstanding in shapeliness and musicality is in fact Parsondes. The transformation of Parsondes is so great that not only does the ambassador not recognise him, he also misgenders him. But Parsondes' condition is not permanent. Once he leaves Babylon, he is restored to his former masculinity and he seeks his vengeance on Nanarus. Ctesias' account clearly demarcates Babylon as a place of gender disorientation and involuntary transformation,[88] a place where femininity naturally dominates, which simultaneously

---

[87] Cf. F 6 = Athenaeus 12.40 p. 530d.
[88] See Haubold (2013a), 91.

empowers women and effeminises men. Even the eminently masculine Parsondes can become effeminised beyond recognition. Later Hellenistic writers engage with this theme, depicting Alexander as corrupted by Babylonian decadence, so that Alexander incorporates the dress of Persian monarchs and embraces eastern luxuries including eunuchs and nightly parades of concubines.[89] Even Alexander, the Hellenistic conqueror of the Persian Empire, cannot escape the transformative effects of Babylon.

The notion of Persian decline and decadence circulated in fourth century Greece, particularly amongst Athenian writers. Plato and the Athenian orator Isocrates presented an image of a steadily declining Persian Empire.[90] Isocrates attributed Persian decline to the socio-political regime and Persian education, whereas Plato attributed decadence to the expansion of the Persian Empire which led to the abandonment of traditional Persian educational practices.[91] Cyrus the Great was always campaigning and as result the upbringing of his sons was left to women and eunuchs. Rather than receiving the rough education that Cyrus had, his sons were instead educated in Median fashion, that is, an education centring on happiness and comfort.[92] This luxury and lack of discipline resulted in 'softness' and led to military incompetence.[93]

Book eight of Xenophon's *Cyropaedia* similarly presents Persian hardness being replaced by Median softness. According to Xenophon, following the death of Cyrus things fell apart; there was infighting, civil unrest, impiety and injustice took over, corruption dominated and the Persians began to indulge in excess and abandoned moderation of ancestors, leading to military incompetence.[94] Although Gruen convincingly argues that book eight of Xenophon's *Cyropaedia* is entirely parodic,[95] Xenophon's epilogue still provides evidence of the Greek stereotypes and

---

[89] Arrian, *An.* 4.7.4; 4.9.9; 7.6.2; Curtius 6.6.1-12; Diodorus 17.77.4-7.
[90] Plato *Laws* 693D-698A; Isocrates, *Panegyric IV and Philip V.* See Briant (2002b), 193-198.
[91] Plato, *Laws* 697c.
[92] Plato, *Laws* 695a.
[93] Plato, *Laws* 697D-698A.
[94] Xen. *Cyr.* 8.8.2-26. Gruen (2011), 58.
[95] Gruen (2011), 64-5 argues that Xenophon engaged contemporary stereotypes only to discredit them by over-exaggerating them with parody and reducing them to absurdity.

rhetoric regarding Persia during the period.[96] It also demonstrates the Greek awareness of the ideological importance of the royal hunt, and how Greek authors presented a king's avoidance of hunting as evidence for Persian decadence. Amongst Cyrus the Great's virtues, Xenophon lists his passion for hunting, which Cyrus deployed as a method of rigorous military training, enduring long periods of hunger and thirst.[97] In contrast, Xenophon describes Cyrus' successors as too weak from wine to handle such tests of endurance.[98]

Mesopotamian Ideology: Royal Gardens and the Royal Hunt

Mesopotamian royal gardens can be traced as far back as the second-millennium BCE.[99] The Assyrian king Tiglath-Pileser I (c.1114-1076 BCE) established the first known Assyrian royal gardens in Nineveh.[100] Tiglath-Pileser claimed he successfully introduced cedar, box-wood and Kanish oak to the region.[101] These trees were acquired from conquered territories and provided timber, a rarity in Mesopotamia, to the region.[102] There were practical and economic benefits in introducing timber-producing plants to the region,[103] but it was also a powerful propaganda tool. The collection of plants and animals from conquered territories provided visible evidence of the king's dominance over these areas.[104] Subsequent Assyrian kings continued to emphasise the fecundity of their royal gardens, as symbolic of their own virility, and also to demonstrate their godlike power to overcome

---

[96] See Sancisi-Weerdenburg (1987b), 119-128 for a summary on the contents and themes of book eight.

[97] Xen *Cyr.* 8.1.34-39.

[98] Xen *Cyr.* 8.8.12.

[99] Wiseman (1983), 138; Stronach (1990), 171; Dalley (1993), 1-3; Novak (2002), 445; Bowe (2015), 152.

[100] Novak (2004), 181. According to Bowe (2015), 152, fn.8 the early Assyrian rulers Assurballit (c.1380BC) and Adad-nirari I (c.1300BC) also laid out gardens but it is uncertain whether they were personal (royal) gardens or productive orchards or vineyards managed by their subjects.

[101] 'I took cedar, box-tree, and Kanish oak from the lands over which I had gained dominion – such trees as none among previous kings, my forefathers, had ever planted – and I planted [them] in the orchards of my land. I took rare orchard fruit which is not found in my land and filled the orchard of Assyria' [trans. Dalley (1993)].

[102] Bowe (2015), 152. The lack of timber plants in Mesopotamia is attested in canonical texts such as the *Epic of Gilgamesh*. Whilst Gilgamesh brought logs of cedar to region for first time, Tiglath-Pilesar and his successors went a step further by actually planting timber-producing plants. On the scarcity of timber in Babylonia see Strabo 16.5; 16.11.

[103] Bowe (2015), 152-155. Argues that the principal focus of early Mesopotamian royal gardens was to introduce and acclimatise plants which would benefit the economy. Cf. Novak (2002), 452.

[104] Foster (1999) provides artistic evidence which shows Egyptian Pharaohs undertaking the practice of collecting exotic animals, which predates the Mesopotamian kings partaking in the practice. The Ptolemies continued to collect exotic animals, with Ptolemy II establishing at zoo at Alexandria.

nature and turn inhospitable desert land into prosperous fertile land.[105] A relief depicting Ashurbanipal II (r.668-626 BCE), relaxing and enjoying the fruits of the earth in his garden,[106] conveys an idealistic vision of the garden as an earthly paradise.[107]

Tiglath-Pileser also established a royal hunting park containing animals from conquered territories.[108] Similar to his collection of exotic plants, the collection of animals demonstrated his control over land. Assyrian kings continued to establish royal hunting parks in order to practise falconry and the hunting of deer, gazelle and most importantly, lions. The killing or taming of a lion, considered the most ferocious animal in the kingdom, was a fundamental aspect of Assyrian kingship as it symbolised the king's ability to protect the Empire and thus proved their worthiness to rule.[109] Greek authors, including Xenophon and Ctesias, engaged with these Mesopotamian models of kingship, using the hunt as a gauge to evaluate the capability of Mesopotamian rulers. Similar to his praise of Cyrus the Great, Xenophon praises Cyrus the Younger's abilities in combat and his love of the hunt, presenting this as justification for his rule.[110] Ctesias also uses the hunt as a barometer of masculinity, praising the hunting ability of Parsondes,[111] whilst presenting weak, effeminate rulers, such as Sardanapalus, as remaining isolated in the palace, explicitly stating that he never hunts.[112]

Mesopotamian royal gardens fulfilled a range of practical, economic and ideological functions. From the ninth century BCE onwards royal gardens were central

---

[105] Stonarch (1990), 171-172; Novak (2002), 452; Novak (2004), 184; Dalley (2013a), 153-179; Llewellyn-Jones (2013a), 93.

[106] BM 124920

[107] Bowe (2015), 158-160.

[108] I formed herds of horses, oxen and asses from the booty I took when I gained dominion over lands with the support of the god Assur, my lord. In addition, I got control of and formed herds of *nayalu*-deer, *ayalu*-deer, gazelle and ibex which the gods Ashur and Ninurta, the gods who love me, had given me in the course of the hunt in high mountain ranges. I numbered them like flocks of sheep... [trans. Dalley (1993)].

[109] Reliefs from Ashurbanipal's II (r.668-626BC) royal garden at Nineveh depict the taming of lions, shows continued ideological importance of gardens continued until the end of the Assyrian Empire. See Llewellyn-Jones (2013a),131-132.

[110] Xen, *An.* 1.9.5-6 Cyrus the Younger fondness of hunting. Cf. Cyrus the Great's love of hunting in Xen, *Cyr.* 1.4.6-15. See also, Briant (2002a), 230.

[111] F 6b.

[112] F 1pd. Conversely, Sardanapalus' successor, the Median King Arbaces, is practised in hunting and war, and is praised for his self-control and noble deeds.

in Assyrian town-planning and became a royal ideological tool.[113] Persian kings and Satraps continued the practices of their predecessors. Typically, Persian gardens were rectangular in shape, enclosed by high walls, surrounded by walkways, and were divided into sections by watercourses.[114] Similar to their Assyrian predecessors, Persian kings collected foreign fauna and flora and boasted of the fecundity and productivity of their gardens.[115] It was the king of kings' divinely ordained duty to restore the earth to the perfect state of its creator before the onslaught of the Evil Spirit.[116] Hence, green spaces were one of the Persian king's most pervasive manifestations of power, and they made sure their gardens conveyed an idealistic vision of paradise on earth.[117] As the next sections show, Greeks encountering these gardens during the fifth and fourth century BCE reacted to them in admiration: adopting Persian terminology and replicating their garden design.

Paradeisos: Hunting-parks and Paradises

The occasional literary references and images available to us suggest that pre-Hellenistic Greek gardens tended to be "enclosed, traversed by a stream and divided into three sections – orchard, vineyard and an area of small plots for flowers and vegetables".[118] These small-kitchen gardens were a stark contrast to the vast royal hunting-parks and luxurious *paradeisoi* of the Persian Empire. Greek interaction with Persian royal gardens led to the introduction of the term παράδεισος (*paradeisos*) into the Greek language. *Paradeisos* derived from the Persian word *pairi-daēza*, meaning wall-surrounded or pleasure garden.[119] The Greek term *paradeisos* could refer to an enclosure, hunting-park or even – in later Christian texts – to the heavenly paradise itself.[120] The word *paradeisos* in Greek is first attested in Xenophon's *Anabasis*, where

---

[113] Comparatively little is known about early Babylonian royal gardens. An exception is the garden of the Babylonian king Merodach Baladan, the contemporary of the Assyrian king Sennacherib. Merodach Baladan's garden appears to have contained non-native species of plant and was structured in a way which suggests it was a physic (i.e. medicinal) garden. See Leach (1982), 5-6; Dalley (1993), 10-11; Novak (2002), 445, 453; Dalley (2013a), 46.

[114] Foster (1999), 64; Canepa (2018), 347.

[115] According to Llewellyn-Jones (2013a), 124 the accumulation of animals, slaves and women, and the display of conspicuous leisure through hunting, feasting, drinking, and celebrating had a major part to play in defining and consolidating royal identity.

[116] Foster (1999), 64; Canepa (2018), 350-2.

[117] Canepa (2018), 346.

[118] Bowe (2010), 219. See also Bowe (2010), 208-215 for an accumulation of these sources which include: Homer, Aristophanes, Aristotle, Demosthenes, Euripides, Isaeus, Pindar, Plato and Xenophon.

[119] Foster (1999) 64; Reade (2000), 200; Foster (2004), 209.

[120] LSJ s.v. παράδεισος

it is used to describe numerous hunting-parks across the Persian Empire.[121] The term is first employed to describe Cyrus' hunting-park at Calaenae, Turkey (1.2.7):

> ἐνταῦθα Κύρῳ βασίλεια ἦν καὶ παράδεισος μέγας ἀγρίων θηρίων πλήρης, ἃ ἐκεῖνος ἐθήρευεν ἀπὸ ἵππου, ὁπότε γυμνάσαι βούλοιτο ἑαυτόν τε καὶ τοὺς ἵππους. διὰ μέσου δὲ τοῦ παραδείσου ῥεῖ ὁ Μαίανδρος ποταμός· αἱ δὲ πηγαὶ αὐτοῦ εἰσιν ἐκ τῶν βασιλείων·

> Cyrus had a palace and a large park full of wild animals, which he used to hunt on horseback whenever he wished to give himself and his horses exercise. Through the middle of this park flows the Maeander river; its sources are beneath the palace. [trans. C. L. Brownson, revised by J. Dillery (2001)].

The necessity of importing a Persian term into Greek demonstrates the distinctive nature of Persian hunting-parks compared to Greek gardens. This was also true for Persian paradises, which were specially enclosed spaces designed to showcase agricultural, animal, and human productivity.[122] Although paradises varied in size, importance, landscape and in their contents, they were all intended to protect specially irrigated and cultivated land.[123] These paradises were powerful symbolic additions to royal palaces: just like their Assyrian and Babylonian predecessors, Achaemenid kings emphasised the fecundity of their gardens, as a manifestation of their divinely-ordained power and their worthiness to rule. Although hunting-parks and paradises were separate entities, the term *paradeisos* was also used for paradises.[124] This usage is first attested in Xenophon's *Oeconomicus* (4.4.13-14), where Socrates mentions paradises belonging to the Persian king.

> Ἔτι δὲ πρὸς τούτοις, ἔφη ὁ Σωκράτης, ἐν ὁπόσαις τε χώραις ἐνοικεῖ καὶ εἰς ὁπόσας ἐπιστρέφεται, ἐπιμελεῖται τούτων, ὅπως κῆποί τε ἔσονται οἱ παράδεισοι καλούμενοι πάντων καλῶν τε κἀγαθῶν μεστοί, ὅσα ἡ γῆ φύειν θέλει, καὶ ἐν τούτοις αὐτὸς τὰ πλεῖστα διατρίβει, ὅταν μὴ ἡ ὥρα τοῦ ἔτους ἐξείργη. Νὴ Δί', ἔφη ὁ Κριτόβουλος, ἀνάγκη τοίνυν, ὦ Σώκρατες, ἔνθα γε διατρίβει αὐτός, καὶ ὅπως ὡς κάλλιστα κατεσκευασμένοι ἔσονται οἱ παράδεισοι ἐπιμελεῖσθαι δένδρεσι καὶ τοῖς ἄλλοις ἅπασι καλοῖς, ὅσα ἡ γῆ φύει.

> "And furthermore," continued Socrates, "in all the districts where he resides and visits he takes care that gardens (*kēpoi) called 'paradises' (paradeisoi)'*, full of

---

[121] Xen, *An.* 1.2.9; 1.4.10; 2.4.14; 2.4.17.
[122] Canepa (2018), 346.
[123] Canepa (2018), 346.
[124] Canepa (2018), 346 argues it was misconception amongst Greek authors that hunting parks were a required part of paradises.

all the fine and beautiful plants that the soil will produce, and there he himself spends most of his time, except when the season precludes it." "Then it is of course necessary, Socrates," said Critoboulos, "to take care that these paradises in which the king spends his time will contain a fine stock of trees and all other beautiful plants that the soil produces." [trans. E. C. Marchant, revised by J. Henderson (2013)].

Xenophon suggests that in this instance the Persian term *paradeisos* is interchangeable with the Greek *kēpos*, a common Greek term for garden.[125] The interchangeability of these two terms is further suggested in Diodorus Siculus' account of the Hanging Garden, where both *paradeisos* and *kēpos* are used to describe the garden (2.10).[126] It is perhaps surprising that despite its reputation as a wonder, Diodorus and Strabo selected the less exotic term κῆπος (*kēpos*), along with the adjective κρεμαστός (*kremastos*), meaning hung or suspended, for the Hanging Garden.[127] The pluralised version (*κρεμαστῶν κήπων*) first appears in Plutarch, and his contemporaries Pliny and Quintus Curtius Rufus similarly refer to the pluralised Hanging Gardens, albeit in Latin (*pensiles horti*).[128] Roman public gardens and pleasure parks established during the early Imperial period were often referred to in the pluralised Latin form, and so it is possible that Plutarch's Greek terminology was influenced by this.

Only Berossus used the term κρεμαστὸς παράδεισος (*kremastos paradesios*) for the Hanging Garden.[129] As a Babylonian priest writing in Greek during the Hellenistic period, it is possible that Berossus used *paradeisos* simply because he was more familiar with the Persian term compared to other Greek terms for garden.[130] However, only testimonies of Berossus' *Babyloniaka* survive, and Stephanie Dalley argues that owing to the lack of cuneiform sources on the Hanging Garden, Berossus' passage on the Hanging Garden was most likely the addition of a later author, whose intention was to provide marvel at a time when marvels were popular with Greek readers.[131] This

---

[125] LSJ s.v. κῆπος; garden, orchard or plantation.
[126] Cf. Strabo 15.7; 16.41 where the term *paradeisos* is reserved specifically for Persian royal hunting-parks.
[127] LSJ s.v. κρεμαστός: hung, suspended; Stalk by which a flower hangs
[128] Plutarch, *Moralia. Al.* 342B; Curtius, 5.1.35; Pliny *NH,* 19.19.49.
[129] Josephus, *Ant.* 10.226; Josephus, *App.* 1.19.
[130] Reade (2000), 200 argues that Greeks used the term *paradeisios* simply because the Persians and Babylonians used this term for this garden.
[131] Dalley (2013a), 35-37. The passage was certainly not an invention of the Jewish-Josephus as the positive portrayal of Nebuchadnezzar conflicts with the typical Jewish presentation of the Babylonian

would explain the use of *paradeisos*, as the term's association with eastern gardens, parks and paradises would presumably evoke greater intrigue and awe in its Greek audience than the common Greek term *kēpos*.

In addition to influencing Greek language and terminology, the Greeks' admiration for Persian royal gardens prompted them to depart from traditional Greek garden design and establish their own parks and paradises.[132] Xenophon built his own private hunting-park on his estate at Scillus,[133] and throughout the Hellenistic Greek world, from Vergina to Syracuse to Alexandria, palaces began to contain their own paradises.[134] Greeks also continued the Mesopotamian practice of acclimatising new and foreign plants to their gardens, which is evident in Alexander's associate Harpalus' failed attempt to introduce ivy to Babylon.[135] The most famous monarchic park was begun by Alexander and completed by the Ptolemaic kings at the royal palace of Alexandria.[136] Thus, there was a noticeable shift in Greek garden design to embrace ornamental, pleasure gardens containing a wide variety of exotic plants and flowers, in addition to their traditional small kitchen-garden.

The Hanging Garden as a marvel

The Hanging Garden of Babylon was regularly listed as one of the wonders or 'must-sees' *(theamata)* of the ancient world.[137] Despite this, only five accounts (four Greek, one Latin) describing the Hanging Garden in detail survive. The surviving accounts date between the first century BCE to the fourth/ fifth century CE.[138] It is unlikely any of the authors themselves visited the site; they were therefore reliant on earlier Greek accounts, most likely by the Alexandrian historian Cleitarchus and/or Ctesias.[139] Four of the surviving accounts (Philo of Byzantium, Strabo, Diodorus

---

king. In the Hebrew Bible Nebuchadnezzar sacks the temple in Jerusalem (*2 Kings 24, 2 Chron. 36*) and sentences Daniel to lions' den (*Book of Daniel*).

[132] See Bowe (2010), 210-5.

[133] Xen, *An.* 5.3.7-13.

[134] Foster (2004), 209. Bower (2010), 217 discusses the royal garden of the tyrant Hiero II of Syracuse whose garden exemplified monarchic extravagance and was amongst the earliest Greek gardens designed for pleasure, with productivity second.

[135] Bowe (2015), 161.

[136] Bowe (2010), 218.

[137] Callimachus of Cyrene, Antipater, Philo of Byzantium, Strabo and Diodorus Siculus all list the Hanging Garden as such.

[138] This is assuming that Philo of Byzantium is Philo the Paradoxographer from the fourth/fifth century CE rather than the engineer from the third century BCE. See Dalley (2013a), 39.

[139] Other possible sources include the Alexandrian historians Callisthenes and Onesicritus.

Siculus and Quintus Curtius Rufus) comment on the structure and scale of the Hanging Garden and the irrigation system that was used to water the top levels of the site. Berossus is an exception, and instead provides a romanticised tale centred around the foundation of the Hanging Garden, which I discuss in the next section. The present section, however, focuses on the Hanging Garden as a marvel in the Greek imagination, specifically in its construction and irrigation, and the scientific and technological explanations that it entailed.

World wonders were "marvels of engineering, construction, technical ingenuity, size and artistic accomplishment", and the Hanging Garden certainly fulfilled these criteria.[140] Until relatively recently, there was a common misconception surrounding the 'hanging' element of the garden, which prompted misguided theories concerning its appearance and construction during the early-twentieth century.[141] These theories ignore the accounts of Philo, Quintus Curtius Rufus, Strabo and Diodorus Siculus which discuss the garden's construction, and describe trees growing on a raised structure, rather than trailing downwards like flowers in a hanging basket.[142] The Greek adjective *kremastos* is better translated as 'suspended' rather than hanging.[143] This is made abundantly clear in Diodorus' account (2.10), where he compares the construction and appearance of the Hanging Garden to a Greek theatre:

ἔστι δ' ὁ παράδεισος τὴν μὲν πλευρὰν ἑκάστην παρεκτείνων εἰς τέτταρα
πλέθρα, τὴν δὲ πρόσβασιν ὀρεινὴν καὶ τὰς οἰκοδομίας ἄλλας ἐξ ἄλλων
ἔχων, 3ὥστε τὴν πρόσοψιν εἶναι θεατροειδῆ. ὑπὸ δὲ ταῖς κατεσκευασμέναις
ἀναβάσεσιν ᾠκοδόμηντο σύριγγες, ἅπαν μὲν ὑποδεχόμεναι τὸ τοῦ φυτουργείου
βάρος, ἀλλήλων δ' ἐκ τοῦ κατ' ὀλίγον ἀεὶ μικρὸν ὑπερέχουσαι κατὰ τὴν
πρόσβασιν· ἡ δ' ἀνωτάτω σῦριγξ οὖσα πεντήκοντα πηχῶν τὸ ὕψος εἶχεν ἐπ'
αὐτῇ τοῦ παραδείσου τὴν ἀνωτάτην ἐπιφάνειαν συνεξισουμένην τῷ
περιβόλῳ τῶν ἐπάλξεων. ἔπειθ' οἱ μὲν τοῖχοι πολυτελῶς κατεσκευασμένοι τὸ
πάχος εἶχον ποδῶν εἴκοσι δύο, τῶν δὲ διεξόδων ἑκάστη τὸ πλάτος δέκα. τὰς δ'
ὀροφὰς κατεστέγαζον λίθιναι δοκοί, τὸ μὲν μῆκος σὺν ταῖς ἐπιβολαῖς ἔχουσαι
ποδῶν ἐκκαίδεκα, τὸ δὲ πλάτος τεττάρων. τὸ δ' ἐπὶ ταῖς δοκοῖς ὀρόφωμα

---

[140] Dalley (2013a), 16.

[141] The most famous example is Sir Leonard Woolley 'ziggurat theory'. See Dalley (1993), 6-7 for a summary of Woolley's ziggurat theory and how it was partially prompted by the misleading English word 'hanging'.

[142] Reade (2000), 200.

[143] Cf. Foster (2004) argues that *kremastos* may apply anything that hangs down, or describe state of suspension without obvious means of support and is an apt word for a carpet garden. Foster considers the Hanging Garden to have been a royal carpet garden as these appeared wondrously suspended and were intimately connected power and prestige. Cf. Dalley (2013a), 16 who argues there is no evidence of a carpet garden at Nineveh.

πρῶτον μὲν εἶχεν ὑπεστρωμένον κάλαμον μετὰ πολλῆς ἀσφάλτου, μετὰ δὲ ταῦτα πλίνθον ὀπτὴν διπλῆν ἐν γύψῳ δεδεμένην, τρίτην δ' ἐπιβολὴν ἐδέχετο μολιβᾶς στέγας πρὸς τὸ μὴ διικνεῖσθαι κατὰ βάθος τὴν ἐκ τοῦ χώματος νοτίδα. ἐπὶ δὲ τούτοις ἐσεσώρευτο γῆς ἱκανὸν ἄθος, ἀρκοῦν ταῖς τῶν μεγίστων δένδρων ῥίζαις· τὸ δ' ἔδαφος ἐξωμαλισμένον πλῆρες ἦν παντοδαπῶν δένδρων τῶν δυναμένων κατά τε τὸ μέγεθος καὶ τὴν ἄλλην χάριν τοὺς θεωμένους ψυχαγωγῆσαι. αἱ δὲ σύριγγες τὰ φῶτα δεχόμεναι ταῖς δι' ἀλλήλων ὑπεροχαῖς πολλὰς καὶ παντοδαπὰς εἶχον διαίτας βασιλικάς·

The park extended four *plethra* each side, and since the approach to the garden sloped like a hillside and the several parts of the structure rose from one another tier on tier, the appearance of the whole resembled that of a theatre. When the ascending terraces had been built, there had been constructed beneath them galleries which carried the entire weight of the planted garden and rose little by little one above the other along the approach; and the uppermost gallery, which was 50 cubits high, bore the highest surface of the park, which was made level with the circuit wall of the battlements of the city. Furthermore, the walls, which had been constructed at great expense, were 22 feet thick, while the passage-way between each two walls was 10 feet wide. The roofs of the galleries were covered over with beams of stone 16 feet long, inclusive of the overlap, and 4 feet wide. The roof above these beams had first a layer of reeds laid in great quantities of bitumen, over this two courses of baked brick bonded by cement, and as a third layer a covering of lead, to the end that the moisture from the soil might not penetrate beneath. On all this again earth had been piled to a depth sufficient for the roots of the largest trees; and the ground when levelled off, was thickly planted with trees of every kind that, by their great size or any other charm, could give pleasure to the beholder, and since the galleries, each projecting beyond another, all received the light, they contained many royal lodgings of every description. [Trans. Dalley (2013a)].

Diodorus explains clearly here how artificial slopes were raised on terraces constructed of stone, bitumen and timber, and soil was heaped upon these terraces whereupon trees were subsequently planted. The other surviving ancient accounts all agree that the Hanging Garden was a multi-terraced system. Strabo describes a series of vaults, Quintus Curtius Rufus a series of columns, and Philo describes a series of columns supporting crossbeams consisting of palm.[144]

The scale of the structure certainly classified the Hanging Garden as a marvel. Both Strabo and Diodorus Siculus provide specific dimensions and claim the Hanging Garden measured four *plethra* each side. One *plethron* is roughly 30m, so this would equate to an area of 120m^2. As well as an unusually large surface area (in Greek

---

[144] Bowe (2015), 162.

terms), the Hanging Garden was a tall structure: Diodorus (2.10) and Quintus Curtius (5.1.35) both claim it measured 50 cubits (approximately 23m) high. Large structures evoked awe, and is something all the ancient world wonders had in common. An epigram from Antipater of Thessalonica emphasises the enormous scale of the wonders he had seen, including the Hanging Garden: [145]

Καὶ κραναᾶς Βαβυλῶνος ἐπίδρομον ἅρμασι τεῖχος
καὶ τὸν ἐπ' Ἀλφειῷ Ζᾶνα κατηυγασάμην
κάπων τ' αἰώρημα καὶ Ἡελίοιο κολοσσὸν
καὶ μέγαν αἰπεινᾶν πυραμίδων κάματον
μνᾶμά τε Μαυσώλοιο πελώριον·
ἀλλ' ὅτ' ἐσεῖδον
 Ἀρτέμιδος νεφέων ἄχρι θέοντα δόμον,
κεῖνα μὲν ἠμαύρωτο, καὶ ἦν· Ἴδε, νόσφιν Ὀλύμπου
Ἄλιος οὐδέν πω τοῖον ἐπηυγάσατο.

I have set eyes on the wall of lofty Babylon on which is a road for chariots,
and the statue of Zeus by the Alpheus, and the hanging gardens, and the
colossus of the Sun, and the huge labour of the high pyramids, and the vast
tomb of Mausolus; but when I saw the house of Artemis that mounted to the
clouds, those other marvels lost their brilliancy, and I said, "Lo, apart from
Olympus, the Sun never looked on aught so grand. [trans. W. R. Paton
(1917)].

According to Antipater, the Temple of Artemis surpassed the Hanging Garden in scale, suggesting that something other than size alone which classified the Hanging Garden as a wonder of the ancient world. The successful acclimatisation of exotic plants in a desert landscape, and particularly its innovative irrigation system, also prompted admiration from Greeks, as well as stimulating technological inquiry.[146] Apart from Berossus, all the surviving ancient sources allude to the irrigation of the gardens, and Strabo, Diodorus and Philo describe the mechanism used for the purpose. Diodorus (2.10.6) mentions a mechanical water-raising device employed to water the top levels of the terraces, but he does not elaborate on the details of this hidden water-raising device:

μία δ' ἦν ἐκ τῆς ἀνωτάτης ἐπιφανείας διατομὰς ἔχουσα καὶ πρὸς τὰς ἐπαντλήσεις
τῶν ὑδάτων ὄργανα, δι' ὧν ἀνεσπᾶτο πλῆθος ὕδατος ἐκ τοῦ ποταμοῦ, μηδενὸς

<hr>

[145] *Anth. Gr.* 9.58.1-8.
[146] Bowe (2015), 164.

τῶν ἔξωθεν τὸ γινόμενον συνιδεῖν δυναμένου. οὗτος μὲν οὖν ὁ παράδεισος, ὡς προεῖπον, ὕστερον κατεσκευάσθη.

There was one gallery which contained openings leading from the topmost surface and machines for supplying the garden with water, through these machines an abundance of water was raised from the river, although no-one outside could see it being done. [trans. Dalley (2013a), adapted].

Strabo (16.1.5) on the other hand, describes the water-raising device as a κοχλίας (*kochlia*):

ἡ δ' ἀνωτάτω στέγη προσβάσεις κλιμακωτὰς ἔχει, παρακειμένους δ' αὐταῖς καὶ κοχλίας, δι' ὧν τὸ ὕδωρ ἀνῆγον εἰς τὸν κῆπον ἀπὸ τοῦ Εὐφράτου συνεχῶς οἱ πρὸς τοῦτο τεταγμένοι.

The ascent to the uppermost terrace is made by a stairway, and alongside these stairs there were screws through which the water was continually drawn up into the garden from the Euphrates by those appointed for the purpose. [trans. Dalley (2013a)].

Kochlia can refer to anything in a spiral shape, and in this instance refers to water screws.[147] Stephanie Dalley argues that the *kochlia* Strabo was describing was an Archimedes screw, even though she locates the Hanging Garden in Nineveh and considers it to be the royal garden of Sennacherib, which would predate the screw's supposed invention by four centuries.[148] Dalley draws on numerous material and cuneiform sources as evidence that screw-technology was available during Sennacherib's reign.[149] She also uses Philo's description of the water-raising device as supporting evidence. Philo of Byzantium refers to a system of spirals involved in the irrigation of the Hanging Garden:[150]

αἱ δὲ τῶν ὑδάτων ἀγωγαὶ τὰς πηγὰς ἐξ ὑπερδεξίων ἔχουσαι τόπων τῇ μὲν εὐθύδρομον καὶ κατάντη ποιοῦνται τὴν ῥύσιν, τῇ δ' ἀναθλιβόμεναι **κοχλιοειδῶς** ἀνατροχάζουσιν, ἀνάγκαις ὀργανικαῖς τὸν ἕλικα τῶν μηχανημάτων περιτροχάζουσαι· εἰς δὲ πυκνὰς καὶ μεγάλας ἐξαιρόμεναι κρήνας ὅλον

---

[147] LSJ sv. κοχλίας anything twisted spirally. From automaton in form of snail to screw, including the scew of Archimedes.

[148] Dalley (1993); Dalley (1994); Dalley & Oleson (2003); Dalley (2013a). Cf. Stevenson (1992), 46-55 doubts the early invention of the screw and proposes alternative forms of irrigation systems, favouring the use of *norias*. However, concedes it is plausible that Strabo describes an Archimedes screw, as he was reliant on alternative sources and it was a water-raising device in which he was familiar. See also Dalley & Oleson (2003), 17-24 where J.P. Olseson argues that the screw was either invented during or shortly after Archimedes' lifetime.

[149] Dalley (1994) 51-4; Dalley & Oleson (2003), 5-17; Dalley (2013), 61-82.

[150] Philo of Byz., *De sept. spect.* In Brodersen (1992), 24.

ἐπάρδουσι τὸν κῆπον μεθύσκουσαι τῶν φυτῶν τὰς κατὰ βάθους ῥίζας καὶ νοτερὰν τηροῦσιν τὴν ἄρουραν, ὅθεν εἰκότως ἀειθαλής ἐστιν ἡ πόα καὶ τὰ πέταλα τῶν δένδρων ἁπαλοῖς τοῖς ἀκρεμόσιν ἐπι πεφυκότα δροσοπαγῆ καὶ διήνεμον ἔχει τὴν φύσιν. ἄδιψος γὰρ ἡ ῥίζα τηρουμένη τὴν παρατροχάζουσαν τῶν ὑδάτων νοτίαν ἀναθηλάζει καὶ ῥεμβομένη καταγείοις ταῖς δι' ἀλλήλων ἐμπλοκαῖς ὀχόν, καὶ βεβηκυῖαν ἀσφαλῶς τὴν φυὴν τῶν δένδρων συμφυλάσσει. σπάταλον καὶ βασιλικὸν τὸ φιλοτέχνημα καὶ τὸ πλεῖστον βίαιον, τὸν πόνον τῆς γεωργίας ὑπὲρ κεφαλῆς κρεμάσαι τῶν θεωρούντων.

Aqueducts contain water running from higher places; partly they allow the flow to run straight downhill, and partly they force it up, running backwards, **by means of a screw**; through mechanical pressure they force it round and round the spiral of the machines. Being discharged into close-packed, large cisterns, altogether they irrigate the whole garden, inebriating the roots of the plants to their depths, and maintaining the wet arable land, so that it is just like an ever-green meadow, and the leaves of the trees, on the tender new growth, feed upon dew and have a wind-swept appearance. For the roots, suffering no thirst, sprout anew, benefitting from the moisture of the water that runs past, flowing at random, interweaving along the lower ground to the collecting point, and reliably protects the growing of trees that have become established. Exuberant and fit for a king is the ingenuity, and most of all, forced, because the cultivator's hard work is hanging over the heads of the spectators. [trans. Dalley (2013a)].

Philo's spirals could allude to a mechanism similar to the one described by Strabo.[151] To strengthen the case that Philo's water-raising device was indeed an Archimedes screw, Dalley inserts the phrase 'by means of a screw', which is noticeably absent in other translations of Philo.[152] The term κοχλιοειδῶς certainly appears to be an allusion to the κοχλίας in Strabo's account, suggesting Philo considered some form of screw-technology to be involved in the irrigation of the Hanging Garden.

Greeks of the pre-Hellenistic period would understandably regard the Hanging Garden as a marvel, in contrast with the small kitchen-gardens and simpler irrigation methods to which they were accustomed.[153] However, Strabo and Diodorus Siculus

---

[151] Stevenson (1992), 40.

[152] Cf. Trans. D. Oates [in Stevenson (1992)]. Streams of water emerging from elevated source flow partly in a straight line down sloping channels, and are partly forced upwards through bends and spirals to gush out higher up, being impelled through the twists of these devices by mechanical forces.

[153] Bowe (2010), 208-9 discusses the irrigation of early Greek gardens. These gardens tended to be laid out on a slope with water traversing the garden through gravity flow. These gardens contained a rudimentary system of water-courses whilst some smaller gardens contained their own well and were watered by hand. Bowe (2010), 216 shows that although these simple methods of irrigation continued in some places during the Hellenistic period, there was gradual shift towards more mechanical forms of irrigation began to occur, especially in the royal gardens of Ptolemaic Egypt and Sicily

were writing during a period when Greek and Roman irrigation methods and technology had surpassed that of the Hanging Garden. Strabo was studying at the Library of Alexandria during the period when the engineers Hero and Ctesibias were based in the city. Thus, Strabo would have become acquantained with numerous hydraulic-mechanical devices in Ptolemaic Egypt, including reciprocating pumps, pneumatic catapults, water organs, and the Archimedes screw.[154] It is likely that Diodorus Siculus similarly encountered these mechanical devices during his time in Egypt (c.60-57 BCE). Even the scale of the Hanging Garden, at least in terms of surface-area, had been eclipsed by the Ptolemaic royal garden at Alexandria.[155] So why did Diodorus and Strabo label the Hanging Garden as a must-see of the ancient world and consider it a marvel?

Rather than a 'contemporary' marvel, it seems that by the first century BCE the Hanging Garden had become a 'classical' marvel. I would like to suggest that part of the Greeks' continued fascination with the Hanging Garden during the first century BCE was due to its association with Babylon, a great civilization that had diminished dramatically by this century. There was also a surge in interest in Mesopotamia during this period in the wake of the first Roman-Parthian War (c.66-33 BCE), when returning Roman soldiers would bring back tales from the region.[156] Thus, both Diodorus and Strabo were exploiting and enhancing Babylon's peculiar mystique in their contemporary audiences' 'imaginaire'.

The lore surrounding the Hanging Garden influenced Greek and Roman garden design. Kings and emperors attempted to imitate and exceed its grandeur. Dalley suggests Herod and Nero had World Wonders in mind when constructing their palaces and gardens. Herod's (37-04 BCE) garden at his Winter Palace in Judea and Nero's (37-68 CE) Domus Aurea in Rome were likely inspired by the Hanging Garden.[157] Both gardens feature pillared porticoes and a water feature for irrigation, whilst Nero's Domus Aurea was set into a garden that was terraced on an artificially created

---

[154] Stevenson (1992), 48
[155] According to Bowe (2010), 218 he garden's area covered a quarter to a third of the city.
[156] Dalley (2013a), 30.
[157] Dalley (2013a), 36. Dalley (2013a), 176-7 argues that although Herod's garden was closer to Egyptian-design, he had World Wonders in mind when building his palaces, and therefore the Hanging Garden was a likely influence.

landscape.[158] This suggests that gardens, specifically, had become hot-spots of cultural fluidity and transmission of influence between the Babylonian and the Greek and Roman world.

Royal gardens and romantic endeavours

The emergence of the ancient novel following the conquests of Alexander further enhanced the reputation of Babylon in the Greek imaginaire, and royal gardens became the setting for sexual and romantic endeavours. The romantic allure of Babylon's gardens is evident in Berossus' account, which is preserved in Josephus' *Against Apion* (1.19).

> ἐν δὲ τοῖς βασιλείοις τούτοις ἀναλήμματα λίθινα ὑψηλὰ ἀνοικοδομήσας καὶ τὴν ὄψιν ἀποδοὺς ὁμοιοτάτην τοῖς ὄρεσι, καταφυτεύσας δένδρεσι παντοδαποῖς, ἐξειργάσατο καὶ κατεσκεύασε τὸν καλούμενον κρεμαστὸν παράδεισον διὰ τὸ τὴν γυναῖκα αὐτοῦ ἐπιθυμεῖν τῆς ὀρείας διαθέσεως τεθραμμένην ἐν τοῖς κατὰ τὴν Μηδίαν τόποις.

> ... and within this palace he erected lofty stone terraces, in which he closely reproduced mountain scenery, completing the resemblance by planting them with all manner of trees and constructing the so-called Hanging Garden; because his wife, having been brought up in Media, had a passion for mountain surroundings. [trans. D. Stevenson (1992)].

A similar account is also preserved in Josephus' *Jewish Antiquities* (10.11):

> ἐν δὲ τοῖς βασιλείοις τούτοις ἀναλήμματα λίθινα_ἀνῳκοδόμησε, τὴν ὄψιν ἀποδοὺς ὁμοιοτάτην τοῖς ὄρεσι, καταφυτεύσας δὲ δένδρεσι παντοδαποῖς ἐξειργάσατο καὶ κατεσκεύασε τὸν καλούμενον κρεμαστὸν παράδεισον διὰ τὸ τὴν υναῖκα αὐτοῦ ἐπιθυμεῖν τῆς οἰκείας διαθέσεως ὡς τεθραμμένην ἐν τοῖς κατὰ Μηδίαν τόποις.

> At his palace he had knolls made of stone which he shaped like mountains and planted with all kinds of trees. Furthermore, he had a so-called pensile paradise planted because his wife, who came from Media, longed for such, which was the custom of her homeland. [trans. D. Stevenson (1992)].

According to Berossus, Nebuchadnezzar designed the Hanging Garden to replicate the mountainous scenery and plantation of Media for his homesick wife. Berossus' account is unusual as it focuses entirely on the romantic incentive behind the Hanging Garden's construction. Curtius Rufus and Diodorus similarly claim the

---

Hanging Garden was established for sentimental reasons: Curtius Rufus claims a Syrian king built the garden out of love for his wife,[159] whilst Diodorus claims a Syrian king built the gardens for his homesick Persian concubine.[160] Neither Curtius Rufus nor Diodorus name the king responsible for constructing the Hanging Garden, although Diodorus explicitly rejects Semiramis as its founder.[161]

Despite Nebuchadnezzar's enduring association with the Hanging Gardens today, Berossus is actually the only source that connects the Babylonian king with the gardens. Josephus' decision to transcribe Berossus' romanticised Hanging Garden episode on two separate occasions is perhaps indicative of the Greek appetite for Babylonian romances during the early imperial period. This is attested in the circulation of a *Ninus* novel, as well as Ovid's *Pyramus and Thisbe* and later Iamblichus' *Babyloniaka*, in the second century CE. Berossus' account of the king's sentimental horticulture can then be better understood in this wider context of Babylonian romantic tales. *Ninus* centred around the romance of the legendary figures Ninus and Semiramis and is discussed further in the final chapter. Semiramis was strongly associated to Babylon, due to her depiction in Ctesias as the founder of the city. Ninus and Semiramis, also feature in Ovid's Babylonian-centred romance, *Pyramus and Thisbe*, albeit in a more symbolic form.[162]

Ovid continues Ctesias' tradition and claims Babylon was built by Semiramis (4.58). He also locates Ninus' tomb just outside the city's wall, even though it was located two hundred miles away in Nineveh. In doing this, Ovid combines these two legendary figures, and places their story as the backdrop to his romantic tale. The forbidden Babylonian lovers Pyramus and Thisbe arrange to secretly meet under a mulberry tree located near the tomb of Ninus. However, their plan is thwarted by the appearance of a lion, which prompts Thisbe to flee and Pyramus to believe Thisbe has been killed. Pyramus proceeds to stab himself (4.119-24):

Demisit in ilia ferrum,

---

[159] Curtius 5.1.35.
[160] Diodorus 2.10.
[161] Semiramis was credited with most building projects in and around Babylon, therefore it is unsurprising some would affiliate Semiramis with the Hanging Garden. For example, Pliny, *NH* 19.19.49 claims the Hanging Gardens were either constructed by Semiramis or by Cyrus.
[162] Ovid, *Met.* 4.55-195.

nec mora, ferventi moriens e vulnere traxit
et iacuit respinus humo: cruor emicat alte,
non aliter, quam cum vitiato fistula plumbo
scinditur et tenui stridente foramine longas
eiaculatur aquas atque ictibus aera rumpit.

He plunged the sword into his groin,
and straightaway, dying, he drew it from the seething wound
and lay back on the ground: the blood spurts high
exactly as when a pipe, split open from corrupted lead,
ejaculates a long stream of water through the tiny
hissing aperture and bursts upon the air with its blows.
[trans. Newlands (1986)]

Up until this point, Ovid had set up the tale as a romance, even beginning the story naming the two lovers as if a title to a romantic love story (55). Pyramus and Thisbe begin as exceptionally beautiful lovers, separated from one another, a recurring motif of the ancient novel,[163] whilst Ovid's references to Ninus and Semiramis alludes to the popular Near Eastern romance circulating in the Greek world at the time.[164] Ovid establishes Pyramus and Thisbe as a romance, only to subvert the reader's expectations in the most drastic way imaginable: death. *Scheintod* is a common theme in the ancient novel, but in Ovid's tale the protagonists actually die. Upon discovering Pyramus' body, Thisbe picks up his sword, and also proceeds to commit suicide.

The vivid and macabre description of Pyramus spurting blood like a broken pipe is erotically-charged. Caroline Newlands discusses the erotic imagery and language of the episode, comparing Pyramus' manner of dying to a gigantic orgasm.[165] But the episode also evokes the idea of water-technology – and since we are in Babylon, arguably the very technology of the wondrous Hanging Garden itself. We have already seen how the irrigation systems of Mesopotamian gardens enticed the Greek imagination. In this episode, blood irrigates the plants, and as Pyramus' blood splutters the mulberry tree, its fruits turn from white to the red colour for which they are now famous.[166]

---

[163] For example, Chariton's Chaereas attempts suicide after he believes Callirhoe is dead.

[164] Mosaics from ancient Syria are indicative of *Ninus'* popularity during the period and is further discussed in the final chapter.

[165] See Newlands (1986). For the erotic language see in particular Newlands (1986), 148-149.

[166] Cf. The myth of Aphrodite and Adonis in Ovid, *Met.* 10.503-738.

Conclusion

The purpose of this chapter has been to highlight and explore the main representations of the Mesopotamian court that will resurface later in the Greek novel. We have seen how lurid and tabloidish plots involving scheming eunuchs, cruel, vengeful women and weak kings took hold in the Greek imagination of the Classical period, especially through the influence of Ctesias's work. These figures will be reincarnated in the novelistic tradition in the shape of the licentious Artaxerxes and his eunuch in Chariton, and the effeminate Babylonian king Garmus and the murderous and vengeful Sinonis in Iamblichus' *Babyloniaka*. This chapter has also shown how the Greek fascination of Mesopotamian royal gardens began with awe for their scale and technological ingenuity. The gardens made their mark on the Greek language – with adoption of a new word *paradeisos* to describe these new pleasure-spaces – and on garden design, but also on the Greek cultural imagination more generally, where the gardens of Mesopotamia were places of exotic wonder, and even more macabre romance.

.

CHAPTER TWO

Mesopotamian Esoteric Wisdom and Methods of Cultural Transmission in Greek literature

The Greeks considered Mesopotamia, particularly Babylon, to be a repository of magical knowledge and esoteric wisdom. The first section of this chapter briefly discusses the origins of Mesopotamia's association with magical practices, specifically astrology and necromancy, in the Greek literary imagination and how through the presence of 'wandering magicians' in Graeco-Roman society, Mesopotamia's association with wondrous activities reached the non-literate population as well. The rest of the chapter discusses methods of cultural transmission in three Greek texts with non-Greek authors: Berossus' *Babyloniaka,* Lucian's *De Dea Syria* and the *Kyranides.* Although these texts cover a range of genres and themes (historiography, religio-cultural and medico-magical knowledge), they all exploit Mesopotamia's association with magic and present themselves as revealing esoteric knowledge, either reaffirming or correcting Greek preconceptions of the region. The narrative strategies I discuss here will be helpful when we come to discuss Iamblichus' *Babyloniaka* in chapter three which similarly presents itself as transmitting Mesopotamian knowledge, engages with magic and lore of the region, whilst also highlighting the complexities of cultural identity under the Roman Empire.

Astrology

Ptolemy's *Almagest* (c.150CE) is a treatise containing mathematical models for predicting movements of the Sun, Moon and planets. It is the only major work on Greek astronomy preserved in its entirety and it became the foundational text for later western astronomy.[1] Ptolemy also wrote the *Tetrabiblos,* a four book treatise on astrology. In his introduction to *Tetrabiblos* (1.1-3), Ptolemy describes prediction as part of *astronomia* and offers a defence of celestial prognostication as more 'fallible yet no less possible or useful than the mathematical prediction of the movements of celestial bodies'.[2] Astrology and astronomy were not clearly distinguishable practices

---

[1] Beck (2007), 4; Stevens (2019), 37.
[2] Stevens (2019), 37. See also Barton (1994), 62.

in the ancient world: in Graeco-Roman society the terms *astronomia* and *astrologia* were used interchangeably,[3] and in Mesopotamia there was no linguistic or conceptual distinction between the two.[4] Astrology, therefore, was not the superstitious art which has come to be associated with it in modern popular culture, but instead was an intellectual activity rooted in mathematical and scientific enquiry.

The most common form of astrology practised in the ancient world was genethlialogy, which focused on celestial configurations at the time of birth,[5] whilst the oldest form of astrology, omen astrology, dealt with discrete and occasional phenomena.[6] Both branches of astrology originated in ancient Mesopotamia, specifically Babylon, where the earliest record of omen astrology dates to the second millennium BCE.[7] Babylonian omen astrology is best exemplified in *Enūma Anu Enlil*, a series of seventy cuneiform tablets dating to the seventh century BCE, containing between 6500-7000 celestial omens.[8] Zodiac astrology, which includes genethlialogy and astrological medicine, developed during the fifth century BCE.[9]

Greeks identified Chaldeans as the ancient astrologers of Mesopotamia, postulating figures of half a million years and more for the beginnings of Babylonian astronomy/ astrology.[10] The historical origins of the Chaldeans is uncertain. Daniel Ogden suggests they originated from Armenia and migrated to Babylon around 1000 BCE.[11] They first appear in Greek literature during the Classical period, where Herodotus (1.181) describes Chaldeans as priests of the Temple of Zeus Bel.[12] The Chaldeans' association with astrology can be traced to Ctesias, who describes

---

[3] See Stevens (2019), 36-39 for a discussion on the terminology of astrology and astronomy.

[4] As Beck (2007), 12 explains, the 'more one knows about regularities and repetitions of celestial motion, further ahead and more accurately one can predict planetary positions and encounters, hence Babylonian astrologers developed as astronomers.'

[5] Beck (2007), 9-10.

[6] Beck (2007), 10-11.

[7] Barton (1994), 11; Beck (2007), 12. See Stevens (2019), 33-93 for a discussion on the history of Babylonian astrology and its interaction with the Greek world.

[8] Beck (2007), 14; Stevens (2019), 62.

[9] Beck (2007), 14.

[10] Diodorus 2.31.9 dates Chaldean astronomical observations to 473,000 years. Pliny *NH* 7.56.193 claims Babylonian astronomical observations have been occurring for between 730,000 and 490,000 years. See Stevens (2019), 34.

[11] Ogden (2008), 78.

[12] Chaldeans also appear in fragment of Sophocles which speaks of man who is 'Colchian, Chaldaean and Syrian by race', demonstrating the interchangeability of Mesopotamian cultures in Greek literature, which is discussed further below. See Ogden (2008), 78-79.

Chaldeans as priests renowned and highly-skilled in numerous forms of divination, especially astrology.[13] In Ctesias' *Persica*, Chaldean priests interpret omens and dreams which encourage rebellions and the overthrow of kings.[14] A notable example is the Chaldean priest Belesys, who encourages the Median general Arbaces to rebel against the Assyrian King Sardanapalus (2.24-28), resulting in the end of the Assyrian Empire and the beginning of the Median Empire.[15] Although in Ctesias Babylon never forms its own Empire, it precipitates all other Empires: the Chaldean Belesys is responsible for the transition from the Assyrian to Median Empire, whilst an anonymous Babylonian dream-interpreter encourages Cyrus' defection from the Medes, leading to the establishment of the Persian Empire.[16] A Chaldean fulfils a similar role in Iamblichus' *Babyloniaka,* accurately predicting that Rhodanes would become king of Babylon, and therefore implying/ encouraging the overthrow of the incumbent Babylonian king Garmus. Iamblichus also establishes a Babylonian persona skilled in divination, presumably astrological divination, further drawing upon Babylon's reputation as the centre of astrology.

Although there is no evidence suggesting that Chaldeans were considered experts in astrology or divination amongst the Babylonians themselves,[17] the Chaldean reputation as highly-skilled, and potentially dangerous, astrologers transcended beyond the realms of Greek literature and influenced Graeco-Roman society. From the second century BCE onwards numerous Roman legislation and sanctions were imposed against (Chaldean) astrologers.[18] This continued into the imperial period, by which point the term Chaldean came to be used to mean 'astrologer' regardless of ethnic or cultural affiliation of the practitioner.[19] This not only demonstrates the impact of the Greek cultural imagination on Graeco-Roman society, but also demonstrates the pre-eminence of Mesopotamia/ Babylon in the Greek imagination when it came to potentially dangerous, or unwelcome, magical practices. This is similarly the case with necromancy, which like astrology, was at

---

[13] F 1pe* = Nicolas of Damascus (Konstantinos VII Porphyrogenetos, *Exc. de Insidiis* 3, p. 4.23 de Boor = FGrH 90 F3).
[14] Haubold (2013a), 93.
[15] F 1b.
[16] Haubold (2013a), 91-94.
[17] Ogden (2002), 33.
[18] See Ogden (2008), 84-5 for an overview of Roman legislation imposed against astrologers.
[19] Barton (1994), 9; Stevens (2019), 34-35.

times outlawed in the Roman Empire.[20]

Necromancy

Greek literature tended to represent necromancers as alien (notably Persian, Babylonian or Egyptian), or as female (witches), or both.[21] The first substantial literary necromancy after Homer is Aeschylus' *Persians* (c.472 BCE),[22] in which Atossa raises the ghost of her husband Darius.[23] Herodotus (7.43) similarly associates Persians, specifically the *Magi,* with necromantic practices when the *Magi* appear to summon the ghosts of the Trojan heroes. Herodotus also attributes to the *Magi* the ability to control the elements and manipulate the dead.[24] The *Magi* were the priests of Zoroastrianism and professional wise men of the Persian Empire.[25] According to Catherine Connors, the *Magi* areas of expertise included: writing; astronomy and mathematics; sacrifice and fire; divination via birds and other media; astrology and the casting of horoscopes (especially political ones); management of crops via manipulating weather, insects, pests, and blight; medicinal and poisonous uses of plants, insects, animals and minerals; topography of marshy delta regions and routes; ritual handling of the dead and necromantic summoning of the dead.[26] Despite their numerous areas of expertise, the *Magi* became particularly associated with necromancy in the Greek imagination. Similar to how the term Chaldean became synonymous with astrologer, the term *magos* became applied to necromancers, even those without Persian associations.[27]

By the imperial period, the functions of the *Magi* and *Chaldeans* had merged in the Greek imagination.[28] As a result, certain forms of esoteric wisdom and magical practices became associated with the region of Mesopotamia, rather than a specific

---

[20] Ogden (2001), 157 argues necromancy was effectively outlawed under Constantius II in 357CE.
[21] Ogden (2001), 128. Ogden (2001), 138 observes that Greeks tended to locate necromancy to the margins of the known world, specifically Egypt (south), Babylon and Persia (east) or Hyperborean (north).
[22] Ogden (2001), 129.
[23] Aeschylus, *Persians* 598-682.
[24] Herodotus 113-4, 191.
[25] Dickie (2003), 28-29.
[26] Connors (2017), 41.
[27] Ogden (2001), 131.
[28] Ogden (2008), 78

culture or peoples.[29] Necromantic affiliation with Babylon is evident in the ancient novel. In Chariton's *Callirhoe,* Callirhoe questions the veracity of her encounter with Chaereas, whom she believes to be dead, suggesting he could be a ghost conjured by the 'magicians of Persia'. Whilst Iamblichus' *Babyloniaka*, which is entirely set in Babylonia, features numerous instances of necromancy, including an instance of apparent resurrection, performed by the same Chaldean man who predicted Rhodanes' future.

Iamblichus' contemporary Lucian features Chaldean resurrecting the dead in his dialogues. In the *Philopseudes,* philosophers from different schools attempt to persuade Tychiades of the efficacy of magic and reality of ghosts, providing a series of wondrous tales [30] Ion the Platonist recalls the tale of the Chaldean snake-blaster (11-13),[31] in which a Chaldean revives a snake-bite victim before blasting all snakes present. Daniel Ogden argues that Lucian's *Philopseudes* makes point of including a full range of stock male magician types, which tend to be chosen for thematic link with their magical or narrative context, and in the case of Ion's tale, a Chaldean is elected due to their association with raising the dead.[32]

Lucian's satirical dialogue *Menippus* also features a Chaldean who is skilled in necromancy, albeit this time in the form of summoning, not resurrecting, the deceased. The text recalls Menippus' *katabasis* to the underworld, where Menippus sought the wisdom of Tiresias concerning the purpose of life. The journey required Menippus to first travel to Babylon to enlist the help of a mage (6).[33] However, Menippus ends up enlisting the help of Mithrobarzanes, a curious figure who appears to be an amalgamation of cultures. The name Mithrobarzanes is Persian, but he identifies as a Chaldean, lives in Babylon, dresses as a Mede and draws his wisdom from Zoroaster.[34] Leonardo Costantini rejects the notion that Lucian accidentally conflated Mesopotamian cultures, and argues that Lucian deliberately has

---

[29] According to Ogden (2002), 33 the terms 'mage', 'Median', 'Persian', 'Babylonian', 'Chaldaean' and 'Syrian' function almost interchangeably in texts concerning magical practices. See above, fn.177.
[30] Ogden (2007), 1.
[31] See Ogden (2007), 65-104 for a commentary on the tale of the Chaldean snake-blaster.
[32] Ogden (2007), 75.
[33] Cf. Homer, *Od.* 10.488-540; 11.13-149. Odysseus also travels to Hades to seeks the advice of Tiresias.
[34] Ogden (2002), 178.

Menippus end up with a 'Chaldean sage' rather than a 'Zoroastrian mage' as a guide,[35] viewing Mithrobarzanes as a parodic figure and his Median dress to be a form of disguise as a Mage and necromancer.[36] Despite his fraudulent appearance, Mithrobarzanes completes a series of rituals which enables Menippus to complete his *katabasis*. Lucian conveys the idea that Zoroastrian *Magi* are purely necromancers and Menippus requires their expertise and aid, yet a Chaldean dressing as a *magos* turns out to be capable of necromancy, enhancing the satirical nature of the text.[37] Although parodic, Lucian's treatment of Mithrobarzanes is less scathing then his treatment of holy men and wandering magicians, who were becoming increasingly common figures in Graeco-Roman society during the imperial period.

Wandering magicians: charlatans and holy men

Wandering magicians provided the Greek-speaking world an alternative access point to Mesopotamian esoteric wisdom and magical practices which incorporated the illiterate population. According to Matthew Dickie, Greek communities in Asia Minor were exposed to the *Magi*, as early as the sixth century BCE, following the Achaemenids conquest of the region.[38] Greek exposure to esoteric wisdom further increased following the conquests of Alexander of Macedon, which led to the development of cross-cultural magical traditions, especially in Egypt.[39] The majority of male sorcerers in the Graeco-Roman literary tradition derived from either the Near East or Egypt.[40] Charismatic individuals travelling the ancient world claimed to originate from these regions and to possess magical abilities, sometimes garnering a following in the process. Graeco-Roman literature tended to label these wandering magicians as either holy men or charlatans.[41]

---

[35] Costantini (2019).
[36] Costantini (2019), 109.
[37] Costantini (2019), 117-8.
[38] Dickie (2001), 28.
[39] The Greek Magical papyri, composed between the second century BCE and the fifth century CE, and the Hermetic Corpus, which was compiled during a similar period, both contained Graeco-Egyptian writings on arcane subjects. See also Barton (1994), 25-8 on the beginning of Hellenistic astrology.
[40] Ogden (2002), 33.
[41] See Dickie (2002), 59-72, 106-111 for a discussion on Holy Men as magicians.

Lucian's *Peregrinus* explores the life of Peregrinus Proteus, who was a Cynic philosopher and Christian at different points in his life, and demonstrates the subjectivity of distinguishing between a holy man and charlatan. Lucian depicts Peregrinus as both a holy man (from the point of view of Christians) but also as a charlatan (from an alternative point of view, perhaps reflecting his own view).[42] Although holy men became increasingly prominent following the emergence of Christianity, holy men were not exclusive to Christianity nor Christian texts, nor were Christians the only recipients of derision. This is evident in *Alexander,* another Lucianic text which focuses on Alexander of Abonoteichos, the Pythagorean philosopher and self-appointed high priest of Glycon (the reincarnation of Asclepius). Lucian scathingly presents Alexander as a charlatan, proceeding to debunk the miracles he supposedly performed.[43] Lucian claims Alexander's teacher was a former follower of Apollonius of Tyana, one of the most famous figures from antiquity, and depicts the entire school of Apollonius as fraudulent.

Similar to Alexander, Apollonius of Tyana was a Neo-Pythagorean philosopher who was accredited with performing miracles. No contemporary writings on, or by, Apollonius survive.[44] However, Apollonius was a recurring literary figure in both pagan and Christian writings well into late antiquity.[45] The short biographies of Maximus and Moeragenes, alongside Lucian's treatise on Alexander, attest to Apollonius' popularity in Graeco-Roman literature as early as the second century CE.[46] But it was Philostratus' eight book biography *Life of Apollonius,* written during the third century CE, which cemented Apollonius' place in the Greek imaginaire. Philostratus was commissioned by Julia Domna, the wife of Emperor Septimius Severus and mother of Caracalla, to write the biography, which recalls Apollonius' travels across the known world. This includes an episode where Apollonius meets the Median king in Babylon (1.25.1). During the period Apollonius was supposedly travelling the ancient world, Babylon no longer existed and the Parthians resided in Ctesiphon. The fabricated episode is indicative of the continued prominence of

---

[42] See Ramelli (2015).
[43] Ni Mheallaigh (2018) focuses on Lucian's critique of magical practices and wonder-working of Alexander.
[44] Apollonius is generally considered to have been active during the first century CE. See Jones (2005), 8-13 for a discussion on the historical Apollonius.
[45] See Jones (2006) for a discussion on Graeco-Roman literature on Apollonius in Late Antiquity.
[46] On early biographies see Jones (2005), 4.

Babylon in the Greek imagination when it came to matters of a magical nature, it is only necessary that Apollonius, a legendary wandering magician and miracle performer should visit a city associated with such lore and wonder.

Apollonius became an icon of paganism and target of Christians.[47] The Emperor Caracalla dedicated a shrine to Apollonius in Tyana, whilst the Emperor Alexander Severus is said to have had an image of Apollonius among his household gods.[48] The Roman official Sossianus Hierocles, writing during the late third and early fourth century CE, used Philostratus's text to attack Christianity in his *Lover of Truth*, prompting a response from the Church historian Eusebius of Caesarea in his *Reply to Hierocles.* In general, Christian writings condemned Apollonius, considering him to be a rival to Jesus of Nazareth Christian texts dismissed the veracity of Apollonius' miracles. An exception to this is the Bishop Sidonius of Apollinaris, writing during the fifth century CE, was an admirer of Apollonius and translated Philostratus' biography.

A thorough analysis on the types and prominence of magicians in the Graeco-Roman world is beyond the scope of this current study, Apollonius is demonstrative of the relationship between wandering magicians and the Greek imaginaire. As a wandering wise-man with purported magical abilities, Apollonius attracted a following and reputation during his travels, and in turn, ignited the Greek imaginaire, becoming a recurring literary figure inciting both admiration and rebuke. Ken Dowden even argues that Apollonius' influence transcended to the ancient novel, specifically in the depiction of the Egyptian priest Kalasiris in Heliodorus' *Aethiopica*.[49] Wandering magicians were a part of a Graeco-Roman society, and in turn feature in Graeco-Roman literature. Iamblichus' *Babyloniaka* and Lucian's *Philopseudes* both feature a wandering Chaldean who stumbles upon the scene and resurrects the deceased, whilst the *Kyranides* also features a wandering wise-man who proceeds to play a vital role in the transmission of the text by translating the ancient stele. The presence

---

[47] For Apollonius' influence in Graeco-Roman society and Christian literature, see Jones (2005), 17-21

[48] *Historia Augusta Alexander* 29.2

[49] Dowden (2015).

of these wandering wise-men In these texts help propel the plot of forward whilst also reaffirming associations of Mesopotamia as an esoteric and wondrous space.

Methods of cultural transmission

The rest of this chapter discusses methods of cultural transmission in Greek texts which present themselves as transmitting Mesopotamian esoteric knowledge through a knowledgeable mediator: either a priestly figure, cult initiate or prisoner of war. Although Berossus, Lucian and the *Kyranides* each view Mesopotamia through a different lens, they all employ similar authenticating-strategies which draw upon Mesopotamia's association with the arcane and subsequently presents the region as containing ancient and wondrous knowledge.

Berossus' Babyloniaka

Berossus remains shrouded in mystery.[50] It is uncertain whether Berossus was a contemporary of Alexander of Macedon,[51] was born during Alexander's reign over Babylon (330-323 BCE)[52] or was writing during the reign of Antiochus I (281-261 BCE).[53] Even his Akkadian name is uncertain: scholars postulate on variations which all roughly translate as the 'Lord/ Bel is his/their shepherd'.[54] This theophoric name places Berossus amongst the priestly elite of Babylon and connects him with Esagila, the main temple of Bel-Marduk.[55] Berossus' precise relationship to the temple remains uncertain. Although according to Tatian Berossus was a priest of Belos,[56] no such office existed in Babylon.[57] However, the priests of Bel feature in Classical Greek literature: as previously discussed, both Herodotus and Ctesias described Chaldeans as the priests of Bel, the latter depicting them also as experts in prophecy and divination. This suggests Berossus was activating this pre-existing

---

[50] Haubold (2013a), 142.
[51] *BNJ* 680 F 1b = Synkellos, Chron. p.49, 19.
[52] *BNJ* 680 T 1 = Eusebius of Caesarea, *Chronicle* p.6 14.
[53] *BNJ* 680 T 2 = Tatian *Address to the Greeks* 36.
[54] The following variations have been suggested: Bel-re-ušu (Verbrugghe & Wickersham (2001), 13); Bel-re'ûshunu (Van der Spek (2008), 277); Bēl-rē-ûšunu (Haubold (2013a), 142 fn, 56). See Stevens (2019), 117-119 for a discussion on Berossus' various names.
[55] Van der Spek (2000), 439 speculates that Berossus might be identical with Bel-re'u-shunu, the *šatammu* ('temple administrator', 'high priest') of Esagila, attested in tablets from the period 258-253 BC. Haubold (2013a), 143 connects Berossus with astronomers of Esagila. See also Stevens (2019), 117 who places Berossus amongst priestly elite.
[56] *BNJ* 680 T 2.
[57] See Haubold (2013a), 146.

Greek association and established a persona to enhance his status and validity specifically amongst his Greek audience.[58]

Berossus is the only surviving example of a Babylonian scholar writing in Greek.[59] His *Babyloniaka* comprised three books and provides a Babylon-centric history of Mesopotamia. Book one opened with a section on Babylonian geography and customs before providing a retelling of Enūma Eliš, the Mesopotamian creation myth in which Marduk saves creation from Tiamat. Book two recalled the history of Babylonian kings from creation to Nabonassaros (747-734 BCE) and included the Great Flood narrative. The final book recalled the history of Babylon from the reign of the Assyrian king Tiglath-Pileser III down to Alexander.

Berossus was writing in a form that was foreign to the literary traditions of Babylon. Ancient Mesopotamians did not write narrative histories like the Greeks. Instead Mesopotamians wrote about their past in epic, in king-lists, in inscriptions (royal or building) and in chronicles.[60] Berossus' *Babyloniaka* was very much a product of the Hellenistic world, intermingling local and Greek elements.[61] Berossus cites his sources, a trope common in Greek historiography, by claiming he had access to ancient Mesopotamian records:[62]

> ἀναγραφὰς δὲ πολλῶν ἐν Βαβυλῶνι φυλάσσεσθαι μετὰ πολλῆς ἐπιμελείας ἀπὸ ἐτῶν †που ὑπὲρ μυριάδων ιε περιεχούσας χρόνον· περιέχειν δὲ τὰς ἀναγραφὰς ἱστορίας περὶ τοῦ οὐρανοῦ καὶ θαλάσσης καὶ πρωτογονίας καὶ βασιλέων καὶ τῶν κατ᾽ αὐτοὺς πράξεων.
>
> (Berossos says ... that) records of many were being preserved with great care in Babylon, which encompassed a period of †somewhat more than 150,000 years ago.[63] The records, he says, comprised stories about the sky and the sea, creation and the kings and the events in their reigns. [trans. J. Haubold (2013a)].

---

[58] Tuplin (2013), 183.
[59] Stevens (2019), 94-143 discusses the importance of Berossus for the study of cross-cultural contact between Babylonian and Greek intellectual culture.
[60] Van der Spek (2008), 279
[61] De Breucker (2003), 31-2. Cf. Berossus' Egyptian contemporary Manetho, who was similarly a Hellenized priest-historians writing a national history composing of three books.
[62] *BNJ* 680 F 1b = Synkellos, *Extract of Chronography*, p.49. 19.
[63] Verbrugghe & Wickersham (2001), p.40 fn 13 claim the manuscript reading of this number is in doubt.

Berossus emphasises the great age of Babylonian historical records and the care with which they were preserved. Although Berossus' figure is an exaggeration, the scribal tradition of Ancient Mesopotamia predates the earliest records of the Greek alphabet by over a millennium.[64] Greeks were aware that compared to cultures Near East, theirs was young and therefore 'indebted to alien wisdom'.[65] Thus, Berossus' claim he consulted ancient Mesopotamian documents would evoke an element of wonder in the Greek audience. The recourse of archives could be a pseudo-documentary strategy. As mentioned in chapter one, Ctesias was the first to write a Persian history from the 'inside'. Ctesias claimed he had exclusive access to Persian royal parchments,[66] but the existence of these archives is uncertain and it may simply have been a rhetorical device to enhance Ctesias' authenticity.[67] However, in the case of Berossus, there is evidence that his claim was not merely a narrative device, but he actually did consult Babylonian records when composing his work.

There is a remarkable convergence between Berossus' *Babyloniaka* and cuneiform sources, including chronicles and king-lists.[68] Berossus also drew on Akkadian epic and Sumerian myth which is clear in his Flood narrative:[69]

τὸν Κρόνον αὐτῶι κατὰ τὸν ὕπνον ἐπιστάντα φάναι μηνὸς Δαισίου πέμπτηι καὶ δεκάτηι τοὺς ἀνθρώπους ὑπὸ κατακλυσμοῦ διαφθαρήσεσθαι. κελεῦσαι οὖν [διὰ] γραμμάτων πάντων ἀρχὰς καὶ μέσα καὶ τελευτὰς ὀρύξαντα θεῖναι ἐν πόλει Ἡλίου Σι[σ]πάροις (...) γενομένου δὲ τοῦ κατακλυσμοῦ καὶ εὐθὺς λήξαντος (...) τὸν (...) Ξίσουθρον (...) ἐκβῆναι μετὰ τῆς γυναικὸς καὶ τῆς θυγατρὸς καὶ τοῦ κυβερνήτου προσκυνήσαντα τὴν γῆν καὶ βωμὸν ἱδρυσάμενον καὶ θυσιάσαντα τοῖς θεοῖς, γενέσθαι μετὰ τῶν ἐκβάντων τοῦ πλοίου ἀφανῆ. τοὺς δὲ ὑπομείναντας ἐν τῶι πλοίωι μὴ εἰσπορευομένων τῶν περὶ τὸν Ξίσουθρον, ἐκβάντας ζητεῖν αὐτόν, ἐπὶ ὀνόματος βοῶντας· τὸν δὲ Ξίσουθρον αὐτὸν μὲν αὐτοῖς οὐκ ἔτι ὀφθῆναι, φωνὴν δὲ ἐκ τοῦ ἀέρος γενέσθαι, κελεύουσαν ὡς δέον

---

[64] Shortly after 3500 BCE Sumerians in southern Mesopotamia began to develop a system of writing, whereas the earliest evidence for the Greek alphabet is the Linear B tablet, dating to the second millennia BCE. See Verbrugghe & Wickersham (2001), 2-6 for a summary languages and scripts of ancient Mesopotamia

[65] Beck (2007), 17.

[66] F 5 = Diodorus 2.32.4 – 34.6.

[67] On the possible existence of these archives and Ctesias' ability to read the documents see Stronk (2007), 38-40; Llewellyn-Jones & Robson (2010), 55. See also Whitmarsh (2018), 41 who highlights the lack of attention over the rhetorical function of Ctesias' royal documents.

[68] On Berossus use of cuneiform sources see: Drews (1975); Van der Spek (2008); Haubold (2013a), 144; Haubold (2013b), 105; Dillery (2015), 138-155; Stevens (2019), 94-143.

[69] *BNJ* 680 F 4a = Eusebios of Caesarea, *Chronography* (ed. Karst), p.10, 17-12, 16; *BNJ* 680 F 4b = Synkellos, *Extract of Chronography*, p.53, 19.

αὐτοὺς εἶναι θεοσεβεῖς· καὶ γὰρ αὐτὸν διὰ τὴν εὐσέβειαν πορεύεσθαι μετὰ τῶν
θεῶν οἰκήσοντα (...) εἶπέ τε αὐτοῖς, ὅτι ἐλεύσονται εἰς Βαβυλῶνα, καὶ ὡς
εἵμαρται αὐτοῖς, ἐκ Σι[σ]πάρων ἀνελομένοις τὰ γράμματα διαδοῦναι τοῖς
ἀνθρώποις (...) ἐλθόντας οὖν τούτους εἰς Βαβυλῶνα τά τε ἐκ Σι[σ]πάρων
γράμματα ἀνορύξαι, καὶ πόλεις πολλὰς κτίζοντας καὶ ἱερὰ ἀνιδρυμένους πάλιν
ἐπικτίσαι τὴν Βαβυλῶνα.[70]

Kronos stood over him in his sleep and said that on the fifteenth of the month of
Daisios[71] mankind would be destroyed by a flood. He ordered him to deposit
the beginnings and middles and ends of all writings underground, in the city of
the Sun, Sippar. (...) After the flood had come and straightaway ended,
Xisouthros (...) disembarked with his wife and daughter, and the captain, and
made obeisance to the earth, erected an altar and sacrificed to the gods. Then
he disappeared together with those who had disembarked from the ship. When
Xisouthros and the others did not come back in, those who had remained on
the ship disembarked and searched for him, calling out his name. Xisouthros
himself they no longer saw, but there was a voice from the air telling them that
they should be god-fearing. For Xisouthros, it said, had gone to live with the
gods because of his piety. (...) The voice also told them that they would go back
to Babylon and that they were fated to fetch the writings from Sippar and hand
them down to humankind. (...) So they went to Babylon and dug up the writings
from Sippar. After that, they founded many cities and temples, and settled
Babylon anew [trans. J. Haubold (2013a)].

Despite Berossus' use of Babylonian dating and terminology (*Daisos*), the
name Xisouthros is the Greek rendering of the Sumerian name Ziusudra, and the
equivalent of the Akkadian Utanapishti or Atrahasis.[72] Unusually, in his Flood myth,
instead of focusing on the survival of human life, Berossus concentrates on the
'writings' buried at Sippar. The choice of Sippar as the place to store the writings was
likely motivated by older traditions according to which this city alone was exempt
from the flood.[73] This implies that the tablets stored at Sippar contained all the
knowledge humans had acquired prior to the flood, which according to Berossus,
humans had learnt from Oannes, the hybrid fish-man creature.[74] John Dillery
considers whether in this passage Berossus was claiming his text derived from the
tablets buried at Sippar, and therefore was tracing his line of transmission to flood
survivors and to Oannes himself.[75] The burying of tablets is also reminiscent of *the*

---

[70] Passage is taken from *BNJ* 680 F 4b (14–17).
[71] Daisios = Babylonian month April/ May. See Verbrugghe & Wickersham (2001), 49 fn.18.
[72] Van der Spek (2008), Haubold (2013a), fn 113; Dillery (2015). Utanapishti features in Gilgamesh
whilst Atrahasis features in another Akkadian flood story preserved on a clay tablet.
[73] Haubold (2013a), 159.
[74] *BNJ* 680 F 1b.
[75] See Dillery (2015), 143-4.

Epic of Gilgamesh, where Gilgamesh buries tablets into the walls or Uruk after returning from his failed quest for immortality, during which he encounters Utanapishti, survivor of the Great Flood.

Although Berossus cites and uses Mesopotamian sources and Mesopotamian tropes, he was writing in Greek and in a form alien to cuneiform scholarship.[76] Even Berossus' autobiographical statement in which he describes himself as a Babylonian priest is a clear engagement with Greek historiography. Such a first-person intervention is typical of Greek historians who present their credentials and methodology at the beginning of their work,[77] but it is a device alien to cuneiform scholarship, which provides little personal detail, with the majority of authors remaining anonymous.[78]

Berossus also engaged with Greek literature by either rejecting, retaining or reworking what he knew of Greek orientalising fiction.[79] This is evident in Berossus' dismissal of Semiramis as the founder of Babylon:[80]

> ταῦτα μὲν οὗτος ἱστόρησε περὶ τοῦ προειρημένου βασιλέως (...) ἐν τῆι τρίτηι βίβλωι τῶν Χαλδαϊκῶν, ἐν ἧι μέμφεται τοῖς Ἑλληνικοῖς συγγραφεῦσιν ὡς μάτην οἰομένοις ὑπὸ Σεμιράμεως τῆς Ἀσσυρίας κτισθῆναι τὴν Βαβυλῶνα, καὶ τὰ θαυμάσια κατασκευασθῆναι περὶ αὐτὴν ὑπ' ἐκείνης ἔργα ψευδῶς γεγραφόσι.

> Berossos gives this account about the above-mentioned king (...) in the third book of the Chaldaika, in which he criticizes the Greek historians for wrongly thinking that Babylon was founded by Semiramis of Assyria and for falsely writing that the marvellous constructions within it were built by her. [trans. J. Haubold (2013a)].

Criticising one's predecessors was a motif of Greek historiography. Berossus accuses Greek historians, which must mean specifically Ctesias, of being ill-informed about Babylonian history and misrepresenting it.[81] Berossus rejection of Ctesias' depiction of Semiramis as the founder and builder of Babylon is probably linked to

---

[76] Also uses Greek rather than Akkadian names e.g. Semiramis (Sammu-rāmat), Sardanpallus (Aššur-bāni-apli).
[77] Herodotus 1.1; Thucydides 1.1.
[78] Van der Spek (2008), 287; Tuplin (2013), 184; Stevens (2019), 103.
[79] De Breucker (2003), 31-2; Haubold (2013b), 106; Tuplin (2013).
[80] *BNJ 680* F 8a = Josephus, *Ant.* 10.7-11.
[81] According to Tuplin (2013) there is no evidence Berossus knew of Herodotus.

the greater importance which Berossus assigns to Nebuchadnezzar, who is presented as rebuilding and strengthening Babylon, as well as building the Hanging Garden for his homesick wife.[82] The episode helped secure a prominent place for Nebuchadnezzar in the Greek imagination.[83] Nebuchadnezzar was the Seleucids' favourite Babylonian ruler, and they affiliated themselves with him: Antiochus I restored the Nabû Temple (Nebuchadnezzar's patron god) in Borsippa, and Antiochus III (223-187 BCE) was presented with the purple robe of Nebuchadnezzar during a visit to Babylon in 187 BCE.[84] Berossus supposedly dedicated his work to Antiochus I,[85] which has led scholars to argue that his *Babyloniaka* was intended to provide a model of kingship for the Seleucids.[86] Considering the apparent preeminence of Nebuchadnezzar and the Greek structure of the work, it is very plausible that Berossus' *Babyloniaka* was intended to provide his Seleucid patrons with models of good Mesopotamian kingship. This would certainly explain why Semiramis, as an Assyrian and woman, was deemed an unsuitable choice as the founder of Babylon.[87]

Whether Berossus was commissioned to write such a work by the Seleucids, or was writing in reaction to the Seleucids and expressing Babylonian anxieties about their rule, remains uncertain. Berossus' *Babyloniaka* reflects the complexities of culture and identity during the Hellenistic period. He engages with Greek preconceptions of Babylon and corrects misconceptions, drawing on Babylonian archival materials. Writing in Greek, possibly commissioned by Greek patrons, Berossus also displays an awareness of Greek literature, adapts himself to the structures of Greek historiography, and even cultivates the persona of a priest of Bel, a fictitious position, to enhance his validity in the eyes of his Greek readers.

Lucian's De Dea Syria

Like Berossus, Lucian was a non-Greek writing about Mesopotamia for a Greek audience in the enigmatic work known as *De Dea Syria*. Here Lucian similarly

---

[82] *BNJ* 680 F 8a.
[83] Haubold (2013b), 113
[84] Kuhrt and Sherwin-White (1991), 71-86. Kosmin (2013), 204.
[85] *BNJ* 680 T 2.
[86] Sherwin-White (1991) view Berossus part of Seleucid effort to revive Babylonian imperial traditions
[87] Haubold (2013b), 107.

employed Greek historiographical devices and established an esoteric narrator to enhance the validity of his text. *De Dea Syria* is a complex text describing the cult at Hierapolis. It is the only contemporary account of traditional polytheistic worship in the Roman Near East written by someone claiming to be an insider.[88] Whether the text is a parody or serious religio-cultural text is a question that continues to puzzle scholars.[89] The narrator of *De Dea Syria* both engages with and distances himself from Greek preconceptions of Hierapolis and Mesopotamia. The identity of the narrator remains ambiguous as his name is never revealed. We do, however, get a sense of his ethnic and cultural background from the preface:

> ἔστιν ἐν Συρίῃ πόλις οὐ πολλὸν ἀπὸ τοῦ Εὐφρήτεω ποταμοῦ, καλέεται δὲ Ἱρή, καὶ ἔστιν ἱρὴ τῆς Ἥρης τῆς Ἀσσυρίης. δοκέει δέ μοι, τόδε τὸ οὔνομα οὐκ ἅμα τῇ πόλει οἰκεομένῃ ἐγένετο, ἀλλὰ τὸ μὲν ἀρχαῖον ἄλλο ἦν, μετὰ δὲ σφίσι τῶν ἱρῶν μεγάλων γιγνομένων ἐς τόδε ἡ ἐπωνυμίη ἀπίκετο. περὶ ταύτης ὦν τῆς πόλιος ἔρχομαι ἐρέων ὁκόσα ἐν αὐτῇ ἔστιν· ἐρέω δὲ καὶ νόμους τοῖσιν ἐς τὰ ἱρὰ χρέωνται, καὶ πανηγύριας τὰς ἄγουσιν καὶ θυσίας τὰς ἐπιτελέουσιν. ἐρέω δὲ καὶ ὁκόσα καὶ περὶ τῶν τὸ ἱρὸν εἰσαμένων μυθολογέουσι, καὶ τὸν νηὸν ὅκως ἐγένετο. γράφω δὲ Ἀσσύριος ἐών, καὶ τῶν ἀπηγέομαι τὰ μὲν αὐτοψίῃ μαθών, τὰ δὲ παρὰ τῶν ἱρέων ἐδάην, ὁκόσα ἐόντα ἐμεῦ πρεσβύτερα ἐγὼ ἱστορέω.

> 'In Syria there is a city not far from the river Euphrates; it is called 'Holy', and is sacred to the Assyrian Hera. This name, I think, does not go back to the city's founding, but of old there was another one and it was later, when the rites became great, that the name changed to what it is today. It is about this city that I am going to speak, and what is in it. I shall tell what customs they use in their rites, the festivals they hold, and the sacrifices they perform. I shall also tell what stories they purvey about the founders of the temple, and how the temple came into existence. I myself that write am an Assyrian; and of the things that I relate I have seen some with my own eyes, while others – the parts of my account that happened before my time- I have learnt from the priests'. [trans. Lightfoot (2003)].

The use of the first person was an authenticating-strategy of Greek historiography and presents the narrator as directly connected with the objects of the study. Only at the end of the text is it revealed that the narrator undertook the

---

[88] Kaizer (2016), 277.

[89] As Millar (1993), 244-5 explains "our entire evidence for the interpretation of the cult consists of retrospective analyses of something conceived of as exotic and distinctly local". Hence, it is difficult to deduce the veracity of *De Dea Syria*. Dirven (1997) views the *De Dea Syria* as a text serious about religion and therefore doubts Lucian's authorship. Cf. Elsner (2001), 153 argues "it is hard – with such a clever piece – not to believe it was written by Lucian". See also Kaizer (2016), 277-279.

pilgrimage to Hierapolis and participated in its rites (60).[90] Thus, as a participant of the cult, the narrator is an initiate who, through experience, possesses knowledge of the cult and spends the entire text educating his Greek readers.[91] The anonymous narrator's identification as Assyrian and his citation of his sources, immediately present him as a non-Greek, authoritative source. Moreover, according to Herodotus people who are called Syrians by Greeks are called Assyrians by foreigners, therefore the narrator, by identifying as Assyrian, emphasises his foreign nature.[92] However, the preface's mention of the 'Assyrian Hera', alongside Lucian's engagement with Greek historiographical devices and decision to write in Ionic Greek, suggests the text draws upon an amalgamation of cultures.

De Dea Syria imitates Herodotus on a stylistic and thematic level as well as in dialect, with the text written entirely in Ionic Greek.[93] This imitation of Herodotus may initially appear to be an authenticating-device intended to enhance the author's credibility. However, *De Dea Syria* was written during the Second Sophistic when Herodotus' reliability was being attacked.[94] Lucian places Herodotus among the false historians dismissing Herodotus' veracity in *How to Write History (42)* and *Philopseudes (2)*.[95] In light of this anti-Herodotean rhetoric, the choice of a Herodotean *persona* for the narrator of *De Dea Syria,* was, at the very least, an ambiguous one, especially if the author was indeed Lucian himself.

---

[90] τοῦτο καὶ ἐγὼ νέος ἔτι ὢν ἐπετέλεσα, καὶ ἔτι μευ ἐν τῷ ἱρῷ καὶ ὁ πλόκαμος καὶ τὸ οὔνομα. 'I myself did this when I was young, and still to do this day in the temple are the lock and my name' [trans. J.L. Lightfoot (2003)].

[91] Cf. In Lucian's *Menippus* the narrator enters the scene wearing a cap, a lyre, and a lion skin, in parodic reference to the mythical figures of Odysseus, Orpheus and Heracles. This odd appearance prompts questioning from his friend, and Menippus reveals that he, like the mythical figures his attire imitates, has just returned from the underworld. Initiation into the mysteries often involved a symbolic descent into underworld in which secrets were revealed. Hence Menippus only reports his experience after learning that his friend has been initiated, presumably into the Eleusinian mysteries (2). The implied sworn secrecy of his friend, entices the reader as it suggests Menippus is going to reveal secret, restricted knowledge, only to then provide a rather humble, banal piece of advice regarding the meaning of laugh: laugh and do not be too serious. The advice, like the text, is satirical, designed to entertain rather than educate.

[92] See Avery (1997), 133; Lightfoot (2003), 183; Andrade (2018), 293.

[93] See Avery (1997), 113-155 for discussion on *De Dea Syria* mimesis which includes; the imitation of language and phrases (113-133); imitation of sentence structure (134-5) and modes of acquiring and evaluating information (135-155). Other texts written in Ionic dialect include Arrian's *Indica* and Lucian's *De Astrologia*. See Avery (1997), 106; Elsner (2001), 127; Lightfoot (2003), 91.

[94] For example, Plutarch's *De malignitate Herodoti.*

[95] Elsner (2001), 128; Andrade (2013), 294.

Jane Lightfoot argues that the imitation of Herodotus in *De Dea Syria* may simply be for the benefit of the Greek audience who would enjoy the presentation of exotic wonders in a literary style familiar and suited to them.[96] *De Dea Syria* certainly exploits the mystique of the east, as the narrator describes multiple marvels and phenomena, including; a head which each year sails from Egypt to Byblos (7), the river Adonis turning bloody annually (8) and the statue of the Syrian goddess whose eyes follow and watch your movements (32). Although the narrator provides a scientific explanation for the river Adonis turning bloody, explaining how it is due to the winds blowing the terrain, the narrator views the wind itself as a marvel, and thus sets aside science in favour of Providence and as a result 'protects' the exoticism of the east.[97]

Imitating Herodotus would certainly enhance the cultural prestige of the narrator and establish him as a man of *paideia*.[98] Throughout *De Dea Syria* the narrator demonstrates his knowledge of Greek culture, as he engages with and debunks Greek myths concerning Hierapolis. These include stories surrounding the original temple's founders, which include Deucalion (12-13), Semiramis (14), Attes (15) and Dionysius (16).[99] The narrator expresses preference for the latter foundation story in which Dionysius establishes the sanctuary for his mother.[100] This listing of multiple explanations before choosing one, is again imitating the historiographical approach of Herodotus.[101] As well as establishing his preference, the narrator also uses this an opportunity to 'correct' Greek misconceptions towards the cult.

---

[96] Lightfoot (2003), 208. See also Avery (1996), 155 *De Dea Syria* 'does not seem to have been designed as a mockery of Herodotus but rather a clever, in part parodic and satirical, mimetic use of certain Herodotean features to describe an oriental place and its oriental practices – a place and practices which might have seemed as exotic to Greeks of the West as did some places described as Herodotus, such as Egypt'.
[97] Anderson (1976), 74.
[98] Jones (1986), 42; Avery (1997), 155-9; Dirven (1997), 166; Andrade (2013), 290.
[99] The narrator reports that the present temple at Hierapolis was founded by Stratonice and Combabos (17-28).
[100] Driven (1997), 164 argues that the narrator gives preference to stories which agree with Greek myths and history and this predisposition is evident in his preference for Dionysius.
[101] Avery (1996), 139. See *De Dea Syria* 11.

The Greeks strongly associated the cult of the Syrian Goddess with fish.[102] They hypothesised that fish were sacred owing to Hierapolis' connection with Semiramis, who reportedly dedicated the temple to her mother, the half-fish goddess Derceto. However, the narrator rejects the cult's affiliation with Derceto on ethnographic grounds, claiming he knows Egyptians who also abstain from fish (14):[103]

> ἰχθύας χρῆμα ἱρὸν νομίζουσιν καὶ οὔκοτε ἰχθύων ψαύουσι: ... τὰ
> δὲ γιγνόμενα δοκέει αὐτοῖς ποιέεσθαι Δερκετοῦς καὶ Σεμιράμιος εἵνεκα... ἀλλ᾽
> ἐγὼ τὸν μὲν νηὸν ὅτι Σεμιράμιος ἔργον ἐστὶν τάχα κου δέξομαι: Δερκετοῦς δὲ
> τὸ ἱρὸν ἔμμεναι οὐδαμὰ πείθομαι, ἐπεὶ καὶ παρ᾽ Αἰγυπτίων ἐνίοισιν ἰχθύας οὐ
> σιτέονται, καὶ τάδε οὐ Δερκετοῖ χαρίζονται.

> 'They [Hierapolitians] believe fish sacred and never touch them... They [non-Hierapolitians] think these practices are for the sake of Derceto and Semiramis... I myself will perhaps believe that the temple is the work of Semiramis, but that it is the temple of Derceto I do not believe at all, since fish are not eaten in certain parts of Egypt, and yet this is not done in honour of Derceto'. [trans. Lightfoot (2003)].

Derceto's affiliation with Semiramis is a Greek legend which can be traced back to Ctesias.[104] The passage is one example where Lucian demonstrates this familiarity with Greek ideas concerning Hierapolis before using the authority of a (fictional) expert in order to correct these ideas. The narrator throughout *De Dea Syria* engages with Greek culture, sometimes rejecting and other times reworking traditions to enhance the status of Hierapolis. The discussion of Phoenician sanctuaries (4-9), for example, echoes Herodotus.[105] However, whilst Herodotus cites the Phoenician sanctuaries to prove that Syrian religions are older than Greek beliefs and therefore superior, *De Dea Syria* draws on this convention to claim that

---

[102] Lightfoot (2003), 65 claims that if there was one thing that "characterised the Syrian Goddess in Greek eyes, it was her association with fish". See for example Xen. *An.*1.4.9-10 which describes a town which regards fish as deities.

[103] Elsner (2001), 135.

[104] Diodorus 2.4.2-3. Dirven (1997), 167-8. However, the name Derceto can be traced back to the Aramaic Tr'th, one of the spellings of Artagatis. See Dirven (1997), fn 71.

[105] According to *De Dea Syria* 4 the Phoenicians do not agree amongst themselves whether the temple of Sidon is honour of Europa. Anderson (1976), 75 argues that the inclusion of this detail strengthens the author's link with Herodotus whose first book opens with rationalised version of rape (1.2).

the sanctuary at Hierapolis surpasses the Phoenician temples in sanctity.[106] The

narrator claims Hierapolis is not only holier than the sanctuaries of Phoenicia and

Syria, but also supreme in ancient dedications, offerings, marvels and divine images

(10).

The cult at Hierapolis is certainly presented as an amalgamation of cultures,

as the courtyard of the temple contains statues of a number of Greek historical and

mythical figures.[107] *De Dea Syria* also emulates the Herodotean (and Hellenistic)

practice of identifying foreign gods with Greek ones.[108] Whilst they share the same

name, the appearance of the Assyrian Apollo is a complete contrast to the Greek

Apollo. At Hierapolis, Apollo is depicted as bearded and more masculine then his

Greek counterpart (35). Assyrians believed images of gods should not be imperfect

(*atelea)*, and they understood youth and lack of full masculinity to be 'incomplete'

(*ateles).*[109] Thus, this is a clear instance of the narrator presenting a Hierapolitian

custom as superior to the Greek. However, this identification of Greek gods with

Assyrian ones also hints at cultural permeability. In the inner part of the temple are

the statues of Hera and Zeus (31). Although Zeus is called a different name at

Hierapolis, his appearance is the same as the Greek Zeus. In contrast, the statue of

Hera looks mostly like the Greek Hera, but also has aspects of Athena, Aphrodite,

Selene, Rhea, Artemis, Nemesis, and the Fates (32).[110] Statues of gods were

material constructs, but they were also cultural constructs.[111] Thus, the fact that the

Assyrian Hera shared features of numerous Greek goddesses but cannot be

concretely identified with any single one, whilst at Hierapolis they worship

manifestations of Greek gods which are the same but different, suggests the cultural

boundaries within which Greeks and (As)Syrians framed their gods were unstable,

fluctuating, entangled and permeable.[112]

---

[106] See Driven (1997), 165-167 who compares *De Dea Syria* to Philo of Byblos' *Phoenician History* which similarly stresses the antiquity of Egyptian and Syrian religion over Greek. See also, Elsner (2001), 130.
[107] Hera and Zeus (31); Apollo (35); Atlas, Hermes, Eileithyia (38), Helene, Hecabe, Andromache, Paris, Hector and Achilles, Nereus, Procne, Philomela and Tereus, Stratonice, Alexander and Sardanappalus (40) Elsner (2001), 141 argues that these statues adorning the courtyard appear as 'Greece's own prized pilgrims to Hierapolis'.
[108] Avery (1996), 145.
[109] Andrade (2018), 308-9.
[110] Avery (1996), 144-5.
[111] Andrade (2018), 301-2.
[112] Andrade (2018), 301-2.

This cultural hybridity reflects Mesopotamian society during the period, and the narrator himself is a product of a multi-cultural society. Hence, although the narrator identifies ethnically as Assyrian, culturally he is Greek and politically subject to the Roman Empire.[113] *De Dea Syria* is a text written by an Assyrian pilgrim (insider) for Greeks (outsiders) about Syria.[114] The result is an intriguing balancing act, where the narrator attempts to assimilate Hierapolis with Greek culture and make it part of Hellenic world, but he also presents the cult as superior to Greek religion and attempts to preserve a separate and unique identity.[115] This reflects the author/narrator's own struggle to establish a distinct identity, perhaps explaining his anonymity.[116] This is perhaps reflecting the suppression of Mesopotamian identity under Roman imperialism, a matter Lucian's contemporary Iamblichus similarly addresses in his *Babyloniaka*.[117] Helen Morales addresses the political implications of Iamblichus' novel and convincingly argues that the characters Mesopotamia, Tigris and Euphrates embody the regions they are named after and that the numerous *Doppelgängers* in the novel is evidence of a lack of individuality and loss of cultural identity in Mesopotamia.[118] Hence, the flight of Mesopotamia to Egypt can be considered a metaphor for Mesopotamian liberation from Roman imperialism.[119] The next section briefly discusses the role of prisoner of wars in Mesopotamian-centric texts (including Iamblichus' novel) and how they are potentially indicative of cultural suppression during the early imperial period. This is then revisited in the third chapter, where there is a particular emphasis on Iamblichus' *Babyloniaka* and how Iamblichus and his text demonstrates the complexities of cultural interaction and cultural identity in Mesopotamia during the period.

The Kyranides

---

[113] Dirven (1997), 164.

[114] Elsner (2001), 128.

[115] Driven (1997), 165-169.

[116] Cf. Elsner (2001), 153 who suggests the narrator's anonymity may be a consequence of his pilgrimage. Elsner questions whether the pilgrimage to Hierapolis is meaningful *because* it strips the worshipper of all his contexts, all his identities, even his eyebrows and hair.

[117] See Kaizer (2016), 278-9. See also Elsner (2001), 147 who considers the absence of the divine name Atargatis (the native name for the goddess at Hierapolis) to be evidence of the suppression of native culture. For general discussion of Mesopotamian identity under the Roman Empire see Millar (1993), especially pages 489-532.

[118] Morales (2006).

[119] Morales (2006), 85-86.

Pseudo-documentary narratives claim, disingenuously, to be based on ancient documents.[120] Often the arcane or inaccessible nature of the pseudo-source is emphasised to enhance the esotericism and therefore the implied value of the knowledge discovered from it.[121] The *Kyranides* involves the discovery of an iron-stele submerged in a Syrian lake, and undergoes multiple stages of transmission, which unusually includes a prisoner of war.

The *Kyranides* is a magico-medical treatise containing prescriptions and instructions for magical amulets and potions. The treatise was arranged according to the Greek alphabet with each letter comprising a tetrad – one plant, one bird, one mineral, one fish with a discussion of their powers.[122] The *materia medica* suggests a Babylonian influence. Babylonian medicine was well-attested by the early second millennium BCE, and the corpus of Babylonian medicine consists of lists of symptoms and *materia medica,* consisting of recipes on how to prepare and administer drugs.[123] There was little in the way of surgery during this period, hence diseases were identified by the examination of external bodily symptoms and were attributed to external attacks on body, either from demons or causes such as bites or poisoned food.[124] *Kyranides* features recipes for amulets to treat a variety of diseases, often involving the removal of a demon or pleasing a god.[125] Early Greek medicine was similar to the Babylonian system, relying on external symptoms and expressing prognoses in the form of signa and omens, but Hippocratic medicine began to depart from Babylonian medicine during the fifth century BCE.[126] According to Geller 'the notion of external attack by demons was replaced by theory of humors or internal imbalance within the human body, which had to be corrected through the use of diet, purgatives, and eventually minor surgery in form of

---

[120] Ni Mheallaigh (2014), 179. See also Hansen (2003), 302 who defines pseudo-documentarism as 'an author's untrue allegation that he (or she) has come upon an authentic document of some sort that he (or she) is drawing upon or passing on to his (or her) readers'. Examples include Dictys' *Journal of the Trojan War* and Antonius Diogenes' *Wonders Beyond Thule,* where the narrator claims to be reporting the contents of a text discovered on wooden tablets found inside a tomb. See Ni Mheallaigh (2008).
[121] Ni Mheallaigh (unpub.).
[122] See Winkler (1985), 263; Ogden (2002), 264. These symbolized the elements: water (fish) air (bird) earth (plant) and fire (stone).
[123] Geller (2010), 3, 13-14, f.n.14.
[124] Geller (2010), 14.
[125] Epsilon (41-44), Nu (103-107), Rho (135-137) in the first book of the *Kyranides* all refer to demons.
[126] Geller (2010), 14.

venesection'.[127] Therefore the *Kyranides* presents a pre-Classical form of medicine, which was more closely affiliated to magical practices than medical theories, emphasising the region's association with magic. Moreover, the pre-Classical nature of the contents emphasises not only the age of the stele discovered, but also the age of Babylonian wisdom and its scribal tradition, similar to Berossus' use of ancient documents.

Composed probably during the fourth century, *Kyranides* as we have it is the work of an ancient editor who conflated two recensions of the same work.[128] The preface contains both prologues from earlier editions of the treatise: the text associated with the Persian King Kyranos and the text associated with Greek scholar Harpokration.[129] Both prologues explain the origin of revelation and process of transmission.[130] In Kyranos' prologue he claims the work conveys revelations of Hermes Trismegistus:

> Θεοῦ δῶρον μέγιστον ἀπ' ἀγγέλων λαβὼν Ἑρμῆς ὁ τρισμέγιστος θεὸς ἀνθρώποις πᾶσιν μετέδωκεν δεκτικοῖς μυστικῶν βιβλίον τόδε.

> Hermes the thrice-great god took this book, a mighty gift of God, from the angels and bestowed it on all people who are initiated in mysteries. [trans D.Ogden (2009].

Hermes Trismegistus was the product of Greco-Egyptian syncretism under the Ptolemaic Empire, as a combination of Hermes, Greek god of boundaries, and Thoth, the Egyptian god of writing, language, wisdom, magic, learning and transmission. The choice of Hermes Trismegistus is fitting for a text which focuses on the deciphering and transmitting of magical wisdom across cultural boundaries. The treatise may draw on Mesopotamian sources and wisdom, but its format and physical structure is Greek, (i.e. arranged according to the Greek alphabet). The attribution to Hermes Trismegistus places the *Kyranides* in the Hermetic corpus, which contained numerous Graeco-Egyptian writings on arcane subjects, both

---

[127] Geller (2010), 14.
[128] Winkler (1985), 262-3.
[129] According to Winkler (1985), 272 fn 34 Harpokration of Alexandria was a famous grammarian, and competent purveyor of a handbook of wondrous remedies.
[130] Winkler (1985), 263.

magical and religious.[131]

The Hermetic tradition exhorted its reader to treat revelations like mysteries.[132] Hence, the prologue of the *Kyranides* mentions that the book belonged to those 'initiated in mysteries'. The reader of the *Kyranides* is initially enticed by the prospect of becoming initiated, and this excitement is further increased upon learning how the text was discovered:

> Αὕτη ἡ βίβλος Συριακοῖς ἐγκεχαραγμένη γράμμασιν ἐν στήλῃ σιδηρᾷ ἐν <λίμνῃ τῆς Συρίας κατεχώσθη ὡς προείρηται ἐν {μὲν} τῇ πρὸ αὐτῆς βίβλῳ Ἀρχαϊκῇ ὑπ' ἐμοῦ ἑρμηνευθείσῃ·

> This book, carved in Syrian letters on a column of iron, was submerged in a lake in Syria, as stated in introduction in the prefatory *Ancient Book*, translated by me. [trans D.Ogden (2009)].

Kyranos claims he discovered and translated the text from a Syriac inscription found on an iron stele submerged in a lake. This is similar to Harpokration's prologue, in which Harpokration similarly discovers the text on an iron stele. However, unlike Kyranos, Harpokration requires the assistance of an old Syrian man in translating the stele:

> ἐγὼ δὲ τῶν γραμμάτων ἄπειρος ὢν ἐδεόμην ἀφθόνως ἕκαστα μανθάνειν· ἐτύγχανον δὲ τὰ ἐν τῇ στήλῃ ἀναγινωσκόμενα οὕτως ἔχοντα.... Ἀλλ' αὕτη ἡ βίβλος κατεχώσθη ἐν λίμνῃ τῆς Συρίας ἐγκεχαραγμένη στήλῃ ὁλοστόμῳ σιδηρᾷ ὡς προείρηται ἐν τῇ πρὸ ταύτης βίβλῳ καλουμένῃ Ἀρχαϊκῇ. ἐν δὲ ταύτῃ τῇ καλουμένῃ Κυρανίδι...

> 'Since I had no knowledge of the writing I asked him [old Syrian man] to teach me everything and not hold back. This is what the writing which he read on the column said... But this book was submerged in a lake in Syria, having been inscribed on a column of tempered iron, as stated in introduction in the prefatory volume called the *Ancient Book*. In this book, which is called *Kyranis*...' [trans D.Ogden (2009)].

---

[131] An example demonstrating this is Thessalus' *On the Virtue of Plants* which recalls young iatromathematician (medical astrologer) who tried to put into practice treatise of Nechepso. After failing, Thessalus searched for the gods and with the help of the priestly elite, was rewarded with theophany from Asclepius. The god reveals that Thessalus has grasped the affinities of stones and plants with stars but did not know times or places plants must be collected. Thus combining religious revelation with botanical and mineralogical astrology. See Beck (2007), 18 on astral lore associated with plants and stones.

[132] Barton (1994), 59.

Thus, the physical text the reader is holding has undergone three stages of transmission: material (*stele* discovery), oral (translation from Syrian to Greek) and textual (*Kyranides* treatise).[133] A wandering traveller discovering a text from extreme antiquity is a common form of pseudo-documentarism associated with 'wisdom narratives' which were often located in Egypt.[134] Whilst in Egyptian narratives priests tended to play a vital role in the transmission process, in the *Kyranides*, Harpokration reveals that the old Syrian man who translates the stele for him, had learnt Greek as a prisoner of war:

> ταῦτα μὲν ὦ τέκνον ἱστορήσας, συνέτυχον τρίτον ἐπὶ ξένης γέροντι πεπαιδευμένῳ λίαν καὶ ἐν τοῖς Ἑλλήνων γράμμασι· ἔλεγε δὲ αὐτὸν Σύρον μὲν εἶναι τῷ γένει, αἰχμάλωτον δὲ γενόμενον ἐκεῖ διατρίβειν·

> 'After exploring these things, my child, I thirdly met an old man who had been highly educated abroad, not least in Greek letters. He said he was a Syrian by birth but that he lived there after he had been taken as a prisoner of war'. [trans D.Ogden (2009)].

Without the Syrian's help in translating the stele, the *Kyranides* as a text (we are led to believe) would not exist. Iamblichus' *Babyloniaka,* similarly features a prisoner of war fulfilling a significant role in the transmission process. These fictitous prisoners of war reflect the real instability of Mesopotmia during the period, but they are also part of a longer tradition of prisoners as form of cultural transmission. Ctesias himself was supposedly a prisoner of war as was Polybius when conducting his history. As prisoners of war who become (at least partially) integrated into their captors' culture, Ctesias and Polybius write their histories in Greek, the language of their own people. The roles are reversed in the *Kyranides* (and simialrly Iamblichus' *Babyloniaka)* where the narrators are the ones writing in Greek and transmitting knowledge they learnt from non-Greek prisoner of wars. The transmission of knowledge in the *Kyranides* crosses socio-cultural boundaries and presents Mesopotamia as a hub of cultural exchange: an ancient Babylonian text is

---

[133] Ni Mheallaigh (unpub.) discusses the materiality of the transmission process in the *Kyranides* and the conflict between Mesopotamian material culture and Greek textual culture.
[134] According to Winkler (1985), 272 there are a number of features wisdom narratives have in common: most mention deciphering a language, exact writing materials involved / secrecy of knowledge they purvey / saving joy it brings / exotic character as something retrieved from far-off land.

discovered by a Persian, translated by a Syrian, recorded in Greek and placed into a Graeco-Egyptian corpus.

The decision to have a former prisoner of war, rather than a priestly figure, play a vital role in the transmission process enhances the excitement from the text. Rather than the narrator intentionally travelling to seek assistance and knowledge from a religious order, it is by chance the narrator encounters the Syrian man, which leads to the revelation of ancient knowledge. The stele was presumably written in an older cursive form, and therefore the Syrian man's ability to decipher the magico-medical text suggests he was learned and possessed some form of esoteric knowledge, placing him within the tradition of wandering wise-men. The Syrian man's status as a former prisoner of war also reflects the political instability of Mesopotamia during the period and the suppression of Mesopotamian cultures under Roman imperial rule. Both the *Kyranides* and Iamblichus' *Babyloniaka* relied on a Mesopotamian prisoner of war to transmit esoteric knowledge, there inclusion may be a subtle suggestion that the continued suppression and imprisonment of Mesopotamian peoples may lead to the loss of knowledge on magical and esoteric practices associated with the region.

Conclusion

The beginning of this chapter highlighted Mesopotamia's, specifically Babylon's, association with certain magical practices and esoteric knowledge. Particular attention was given to astrology and necromancy, due to their pre-eminence in the Greek imaginaire of Babylon and presence in the ancient novel. Similarly, wandering magicians were briefly discussed in order to highlight an alternative way the Greek-speaking world encountered Mesopotamian magical practices which in turn influenced Graeco-Roman literature. The majority of the chapter explored methods of cultural transmission and how non-Greek authors exploited the association of Mesopotamia/ Babylon with magical practices and ancient wisdom to present themselves as revealing esoteric knowledge from the region. Berossus, Lucian and the *Kyranides* all employed authenticating devices to enhance their validity and used this platform to rework Greek traditions or challenge preconceptions whilst also addressing the complexities of cultural identity during the period. We shall see in the next chapter how Iamblichus's *Babyloniaka* combined the numerous narrative devices discussed in this chapter, including establishing a local, esoteric narrator skilled in divination and relying on a prisoner of war for the transmission of knowledge, and in doing so, enhanced the reputation of Babylon as a wondrous and magical space.

CHAPTER THREE

Babylon in the Novelistic Tradition

The rise of the ancient novel in the wake of Alexander the Great's expeditions further enriched the reputation of Babylon in the Greek imaginaire. This chapter primarily focuses on two ancient novels: Chariton' *Callirhoe* and Iamblichus' *Babyloniaka*. These novels embody the different strands discussed in the previous chapters, presenting the exoticism of the political and natural world alongside the secret lore and esotericism of Babylon. The purpose of this chapter is twofold: firstly to demonstrate how Babylon acted as a liminal space in Greek literature, where historiography and romance merged and the boundaries between history and fiction became distorted, and secondly, to discuss the depiction of Babylon in the novelistic tradition, and how the city was depicted as a highly-eroticised, dangerous and unstable space.

Mesopotamian romances outside the ancient novel

Defining the genre of the ancient novel is a complex and nuanced subject.[1] Broadly speaking, we can attribute two key features to the ancient novel: young, heterosexual reciprocal love at first sight and the theme of travel, which includes separation and multiple ordeals before the successful return home (*nostos*).[2] Novelistic romances always conclude with the marriage, or re-establishment of marriage, of the protagonists.[3] Conversely, romantic endeavours depicted outside the novelistic tradition are more prone to tragedy, either in the form of unreciprocated love and/or death. This is the case in Ctesias' *Persica* and Xenophon's *Cyropaedia* which feature notable, but tragic, romances. Both texts are considered forerunners to the ancient novel, and provide evidence that erotic Mesopotamian-centric romances existed, and pre-existed, Hellenocentric romances adopted by ancient novelists.[4]

---

[1] See Selden (1993); Goldhill (2008) for a discussion on the intricacies and complexities involved in defining the genre of the ancient novel.
[2] Whitmarsh (2011), 6, 14-15; Whitmarsh (2018), 12. On travel in the novel see Romm (2008).
[3] Whitmarsh (2018), 12.
[4] Whitmarsh (2018), 33.

Xenophon's biography of Cyrus the Great has been dubbed a 'romanticised biography'.[5] This is largely due to the romance of Abradates and Panthea, which plays a significant part in the second half of Xenophon's *Cyropaedia.*[6] The tragic romance culminates with the death of Abradates in battle and Panthea's subsequent grief-stricken suicide.[7] Abradates and Panthea became recurring literary figures, reappearing in comic and tragic romances. Their romance became a well-known tale, even to those who had never read Xenophon.[8] Panthea's fidelity and subsequent suicide is the sort of behaviour one would expect from a novelistic heroine. The threat of, or attempted, suicide by the hero or heroine following the separation (or threatened separation) from their lover was a common theme of the ancient novel. In Iamblichus' *Babyloniaka,* Sinonis even attempts to kill herself by her own sword, echoing Panthea's noble act.

Ctesias similarly includes episodes in which characters act in a way we would consider typical novelistic behaviour. Ctesias' *Persica* combines elements of history and fiction, leading to the terms 'romantic historiography' and 'fictional historiography' being applied to the text.[9] Similar to Xenophon's tragic romance, Ctesias' love story of the Median general Styrangaeus and the Scythian warrior-Queen Zarinaea ends with suicide. Stryangaeus kills himself following Zarinaea's rejection of their union on political grounds, although ironically, his death results in a political alliance between the Medes and Scythians.[10] Only a single papyrus, 29 lines in length survives from Ctesias' *Persica,* and it reports the letter sent by Styrangaeus to Zarinaea following her rejection of him:[11]

/ [.]ạ.σ.[.].λε.απαγψ.τες δ' ἐ[σ]/τιν ὅτι ἅγος ἐνέλειπες'. ὁ δ' εἶ/πεν· 'φέρε τὸ γοῦν πρῶτον / [γ]ράμματα [γ]ράψω πρὸς Ζαρει/εναίαν (?)'. καὶ γράφει· Στρυαγ/γαῖος Ζαρε[ιεν]αίαι οὕτω λέγει· / ἐγὼ μὲν σὲ ἔσωσα, καὶ σὺ δι' ἐ/μὲ ἐσ[ώ]θης, ἐγὼ δὲ διὰ σὲ ἀ/πω[λ]όμην, καὶ ἀπέκτεινα / αὐτὸς ἐμαυτόν· οὐ γάρ μοι σὺ ἐ/βούλου χαρ[ί]σασθαι. ἐγὼ δὲ ταῦ/τα τὰ κακὰ καὶ τὸν ἔρωτα τόν/δε

---

[5] Hagg (1987), 193.
[6] Xen. Cyr. 4.6.11, 5.1.2–18, 6.1.45–51, 6.4.1–11, 7.1.29–32, 7.3.2–16.
[7] Xen *Cyr.* 7.3.14-5.
[8] According to Tatum (1989), 20, similar to the story of Cupid and Psyche in Apuleius' *Golden Ass,* Abradates and Panthea became a well-known tale to those who had never read Xenophon.
[9] On the genre of Ctesias' *Persica* see Marincola (1997), 22; Briant (2002), 272; Stronk (2004-5), pp; Stronk (2007), 43-55; Whitmarsh (2008), 2; Llewellyn-Jones & Robson (2010), 68-80; Wieshöfer (2013), 137-141; Whitmarsh (2018), 43-5.
[10] See also, F 8c = Nicolas of Damascus (*Exc. de Virtutbus* p. 335.20 Büttner-Wobst = FGrH 90 F5)
[11] F 8b = POxy 2330.

οὐκ αὐτὸς εἱλόμην, ὁ δὲ θεὸς / οὗτό[ς] ἐστιν κοινὸς καὶ σοὶ καὶ / ἅπασιν ἀνθρώποισιν. ὅτωι μὲν οὖν εἴλεως ἔλθηι, πλεί/στας γε ἡδονὰς δίδωσιν, καὶ ἄλλα πλεῖστα ἀγαθὰ ἐποίησεν αὐ/τόν, ὅτωι δὲ ὀργιζόμενος / ἔλθη<ι> ο[ἷον]περ ἐμοὶ νῦν, πλεῖ/στα κ[ακὰ ἐρ]γασάμενος τὸ τελευ/ταῖον πρόρριζον ἀπώλεσεν / καὶ ἐξέτ[ρ]εψεν. τεκμαίρομαι / δὲ τῶι ἐμῶι θανάτωι. [ἐ]γὼ / γάρ σοι καταράσομαι μὲν οὐ/δέν, ἐπεύξομαι δέ σοι τὴν / δικαιο[τ]ά[τ]ην εὐχήν· εἰ μὲν σὺ ἐμὲ [δ]ίκ[α]ια ἐποίησας, πολ**

Styrangaeus writes to Zarinaea as follows: I saved you; it was through me that you were saved. But it was through you that I was destroyed; and I have killed myself, for you were unwilling to return my feelings. I did not myself choose these ills and this desire; this god is common to you, and to the whole human race. He gives the greatest number of pleasures to anyone on whom he comes favourably, and does him the greatest good; but to anyone on whom he visits his anger, as he does on me now, he causes the greatest trouble, and finally destroys him root-and-branch, and overturns him. I bear witness to this by my own death. I do not curse you at all, rather I shall offer the most just prayer for you: if you treated me justly… [papyrus breaks off]. [trans. Whitmarsh (2018)].

Styrangaeus' despair, reproachful letter writing and threatened suicide, are all recurring themes in the ancient novel.[12] Whitmarsh also draws attention to the linguistic and stylistic similarities between Styrangaeus' letter and Chaereas' lament over Callirhoe (4.3), suggesting that Chariton knew, and drew upon, Ctesias' *Persica*. Indeed Chariton' decision to set his novel during the reign of Artaxerxes II, the presence of Stateira, Mithridates, Megabyzus, Rhodogyne, Zopyrus and Pharnaces in his novel, and his depiction of a licentious and weak king in Babylon, certainly suggests Ctesias influenced Chariton.[13] These two examples demonstrate that certain novelistic behaviours and motifs pre-existed the ancient novel and Mesopotamia was at the centre of the development of certain traditions.

Early Greek novels

Early Greek novelists placed historical and legendary Mesopotamian figures at the centre of romantic episodes, blurring the distinction between history and fiction. This is most apparent with the figures of Ninus and Semiramis, whom Ctesias presents as the founders of the Assyrian Empire and therefore at the beginning of

---

[12] For a discussion on the novelistic motifs present in Ctesias' Styrangaeus and Zarinaea, see Whitmarsh (2018), 33-38.

[13] Ctesias was the physician at the court Artaxerxes II, whilst the mentioned Persian figures all feature in his *Persica*.

Mesopotamian history.[14] Ctesias depicts Semiramis as the daughter of half-fish goddess Derceto and as the founder of Babylon. Semiramis was loosely based on the Assyrian Queen Šammu-ramāt' (r. 823 to 810 BCE).[15] Although Šammu-ramāt's main royal residence was at Nimrud,[16] Semiramis became affiliated with Babylon as the city's fonder, builder of its walls and, in some traditions, the construction of the Hanging Garden.[17] Conversely, Ninus became affiliated with Nineveh. Unlike Semiramis, there is no cuneiform evidence for Ninus, suggesting he was purely a fictional creation of Ctesias.[18] Despite the fictionality of Ninus, the Assyrian king continued to be associated with Semiramis in Greek literature: subsequent Greek and Roman histories began with the reign of Ninus and Semiramis and the legendary couple became romanticised figures.[19]

The popularity of Ninus and Semiramis is evident in two mosaics, one in a villa near Antioch and the other in Alexandretta, depicting scenes from a romance of the couple.[20] These scenes are considered to be inspired by episodes from the fragmentary romance *Ninus*. The *Ninus* papyrus dates to the mid to late first century CE.[21] The papyrus depicts a couple of young, frustrated but virtuous lovers who are often identified as Ninus and Semiramis.[22] Ancient novels centred around wholly-invented characters (not mythical or historical),[23] therefore the presence of Ninus and Semiramis has led to the suggestion that the text may have been embedded in a

---

[14] Pompeius Trogus begins his history with Semiramis and Ninus. The lost works of Dinon and Clitarchus used and adapted Ctesias' work and may have transformed Ninus and Semiramis into central personae. See Stronk (2016), 529-30.

[15] Sammu-Ramat was the ninth century BCE daughter-in-law of Shalmaneser III, wife of Shamshi-Adad V and mother of Adad-nirari III. See Dalley (2013a), 117-122; Stephens (2014), 152; Stronk (2016), 526-7; Whitmarsh (2018), 163.

[16] Dalley (2013a), 118.

[17] Pliny, *NH* 19.19.49 claims the Hanging Gardens were either constructed by Semiramis or by Cyrus. Diodorus 2.10 claims a Syrian king built the gardens for his homesick Persian concubine and specifically rejects Semiramis as founder, suggesting a pre-existing tradition associating Sermiamis with the Hanging Garden existed.

[18] Dalley (2013a), 121; Stephens (2014), 152; Whitmarsh (2018),163.

[19] How romanticised Ctesias' account on Ninus and Semiramis was is unknown due to our reliance on Diodorus' epitome and Diodorus' tendency to exclude erotic episodes, such as Styrangaeus and Zarinaea. See Whitmarsh (2018), 163-4.

[20] Stephens and Winkler (1995), 24; Dalley (2013a), 124; Stephens (2014), 151. *Metiochus and Parthenope* is the only other ancient novel to capture the imagination enough to become subject for visual depiction.

[21] Stephens & Winkler (1995), 23; Whitmarsh (2018), 161.

[22] Whitmarsh (2018), 161-2.

[23] Whitmarsh (2008), 3

historical or a biographical account,[24] possibly a '*Ninopaeidia*' of sorts.[25] However, the figures in the papyrus display behaviour typical of novelistic heroes and heroines, which sharply contrasts to the usual depiction of Ninus and Semiramis. Although Hellenistic sources, such as the poems of Euphorion, indicate that the Greek romanticisation of Semiramis predated the *Ninus* papyrus, she was not 'Hellenized' in the same manner.[26] Susan Stephens addresses the *Ninus* papyrus' adaptation of Ninus and Semiramis from the world conquerors we see in Greek histories into "Greek youths, respectful of their elders, speaking in polished rhetorical periods, and adapted to Greek cultural norms".[27] The formidable Semiramis, leader of armies and founder of Babylon, becomes an unrecognisably shy and tongue-tied girl, confined to the women's quarters and too embarrassed to admit to her aunt she is in love with her cousin.[28] The inclusion of legendary Mesopotamian figures in romantic episodes evidently provided enjoyment for Greek audiences, whilst the Hellenization of these characters made them more accessible for Greek readership, placing unfamiliar and obscure characters in a familiar setting.

By the early imperial period specifically Babylonian, rather than Mesopotamian, romantic endeavours were popular outside the novelistic tradition as well. In the first chapter we discussed the increasing intrigue and wonder of Babylon during the early imperial period, specifically with regard to the Hanging Garden. Ovid's *Pyramus and Thisbe* was a tragic Babylonian romance which symbolically places Ninus and Semiramis at its centre, whilst the circulation of Berossus-via-Josephus' romantic episode on the construction of the Hanging Garden attests to the popularity of such narratives during the period.[29] The rest of the chapter will discuss how the novelists Chariton and Iamblichus expanded upon pre-existing Greek

---

[24] Whitmarsh (2018), 162. Hence, Hagg refrains from labelling *Ninus* a historical novel. See Hagg (1987), fn. 78.

[25] Stephens and Winkler (1995), 26.

[26] According to Visscher (2020), 184-6, Euphorion mentions Semiramis on at least two separate occasions and in both instances focuses on romantic elements rather than her statesmanship.

[27] Stephens (2008), 68. See also Stephens (2014), 151.

[28] Stephens (2008), 68; Stephens (2014), 151. Cf. Whitmarsh (2018), 164 argues that the shy girl of the *Ninus* papyrus is such a contrast to the warrior-Queen Semiramis, that the girl from the papyrus cannot possibly be Semiramis. However, Stephens (2014), 151 argues that mother's name is Derkeia, which is clearly alluding to Derceto, which suggests the fictional heroine was indeed Semiramis.

[29] For a discussion on royal gardens as a choice of setting for romantic endeavours, and an analysis on Ovid's *Pyramus and Thisbe*, please refer to the first chapter.

traditions of Babylon, combining the image of a sensationalised court with the lore and magic associated with the region to produce an image of a licentious, dangerous and unstable Babylon in the Greek reader's imagination.

Chariton's *Callirhoe*

The majority of the plot of Chariton's *Callirhoe* takes place within the Persian Empire and the novel is structured around Chaereas' and Callirhoe's journey to and from Babylon. [30] Callirhoe's crossing of the river Euphrates (5.1) marks the narrative transition from west to east.[31] The significance of this moment is impossible to miss as Callirhoe performs a soliloquy lamenting *Fortuna* and the crossing of the river.[32]

"Τύχη βάσκανε, κατὰ μιᾶς γυναικὸς προσφιλονικοῦσα πολέμῳ...
νῦν δὲ ἔξω με τοῦ συνήθους ῥίπτεις ἀέρος καὶ τῆς
πατρίδος ὅλῳ διορίζομαι κόσμῳ. Μίλητον ἀφείλω μου πάλιν,
ὡς πρότερον Συρακούσας· ὑπὲρ τὸν Εὐφράτην ἀπάγομαι καὶ
βαρβάροις ἐγκλείομαι μυχοῖς ἡ νησιῶτις, ὅπου μηκέτι θάλασσα...
ἅπαξ, Εὐφρᾶτα, μέλλω σε διαβαίνειν· φοβοῦμαι γὰρ οὐχ οὕτω
τὸ μῆκος τῆς ἀποδημίας ὡς μὴ δόξω τινὶ κἀκεῖ καλή." ταῦτα
ἅμα λέγουσα τὴν γῆν κατεφίλησεν, εἶτα ἐπιβᾶσα τῆς πορθμίδος διεπέρασεν.

"Malicious Fortune! Insistently attacking a lone woman!... Now you are hurling me from my familiar world – I am at the other end of the earth from my own country. This time it is Miletus you have taken from me; before, it was Syracuse. I am being taken beyond the Euphrates, shut up in the depths of barbarian lands where the sea is far away – I, an island woman!... Only once, Euphrates, am I going to cross you – it is not the length of the journey that frightens me, but the fear that there too someone will think me beautiful!" With these words she kissed the ground, stepped on board the ferry, and crossed the river.

Callirhoe believes she is leaving her past and the Greek world of Syracuse behind, and the crossing of the river symbolises the next stage of life. The recap of events at the beginning of book five suggests a new scroll would begin,[33] making the

---

[30] Book one takes place is Syracuse, book two is set in Miletus, book three recalls Chaereas' journey eastwards, book four recalls Callirhoe's journey east, book five is in Babylon, book six describes Callirhoe journey away from the east, book seven Chaereas' journey away from east, and book eight recalls Chaereas and Callirhoe journey back to Syracuse, marking the completion of the protagonists' *nostos* where they find themselves in the same position as book one.

[31] Schwartz (2003), 389 considers Miletus to be a liminal space between east and west.

[32] The role of the river Euphrates as a boundary is later reaffirmed when Chaereas and Polymarchus cross over it (7.2). Callirhoe feels she is leaving her past and Syracuse behind, and the crossing of the river symbolising the next stage of life. Whitmarsh (2009), 43. compares the river crossing to book five of Achilles Tatius novel where the arrival in Alexandria marks the new beginning for protagonists

[33] Whitmarsh (2009), 36-50; Holzberg (1995), 44.

significance of the river crossing unmissable due to the physicality involved in putting down one scroll and picking up the next. Babylon is structurally the midpoint of the novel.[34] It marks the brief reunion between Chaereas and Callirhoe, and it is here that their love faces their biggest obstacle yet: the Persian king Artaxerxes II.

Dionysius attempts to keep Callirhoe concealed in Babylon, fearing she would attract unwanted attention in a 'city full of men like Mithridates' (5.2). Little did he realise that Callirhoe would end up attracting the attention of the king himself.[35] Artaxerxes first encounters Callirhoe whilst presiding over the trial for her marriage (5.8). After the revelation that Chaereas is alive, the trial is postponed and Callirhoe is escorted to the royal palace, where she is entrusted to the care of Statira, Artaxerxes' wife (5.9). Chariton briefly alludes to magical practices associated with Babylon as Callirhoe contemplates her encounter with Chaereas. Prior to entering Babylon, Callirhoe believed Chaereas to be dead,[36] and therefore she questions whether she had really seen Chaereas or a ghost conjured by the 'magicians of Persia' (5.9).

> "εἴδετε" φησὶ "Χαιρέαν ὑμεῖς ἀληθῶς; ἐκεῖνος ἦν Χαιρέας ὁ ἐμός, ἢ καὶ
> φησὶ "Χαιρέαν ὑμεῖς ἀληθῶς; ἐκεῖνος ἦν Χαιρέας ὁ ἐμός, ἢ καὶ
> τοῦτο πεπλάνημαι; τάχα γὰρ Μιθριδάτης διὰ τὴν δίκην εἴδωλον ἔπεμψε·
> λέγουσι γὰρ ἐν Πέρσαις εἶναι μάγους. ἀλλὰ καὶ ἐλάλησε καὶ πάντα εἶπεν ὡς
> εἰδώς. πῶς οὖν ὑπέμεινέ μοι μὴ περιπλακῆναι; μηδὲ καταφιλήσαντες
> ἀλλήλους διελύθημεν."

> "Have you really seen Chaereas?" she said. "Was that my Chaereas? Or is that too an illusion? Perhaps Mithridates called up a spirit from the trial; they say there are magicians in Persia.[37] But he actually spoke – everything he said showed he knew the situation. Then how could he bear not to embrace me? We parted without even a kiss!"

As the reader we know that Chaereas is alive, debunking any potential wonder from the episode, which, as we shall see, contrasts to Iamblichus' novel. Chariton focuses less on the magic and supernatural aspects of Babylon and instead

---

[34] Whitmarsh (2009), 39, 42 fn.26.

[35] Llewellyn-Jones (2013b), 169 describes Callirrhoe's journey from Miletus to Babylon as an 'erotic *Anabasis*', noting how Callirhoe becomes the obsession of increasingly powerful men, from Dionysius, to the Satraps Mithridates and Pharnaces, and culminating with the king himself.

[36] Callirhoe had even created a burial mound for Chaereas in Miletus (4.1).

[37] This is undoubtedly a reference to the *Magi*, the fire priests of Persia whom the Greeks associated with necromantic practices. See chapter two.

concentrates on the political intrigue and eroticism of the city, focusing on
Artaxerxes' pursuit of Callirhoe during her stay there.

Licentious kings

Initially Artaxerxes demonstrates restraint over his passion for Callirhoe.
Artaxerxes confides in his most trusted eunuch Artaxates, confessing his burning
desire for Callirhoe but his unwillingness to pursue the wife of another man.
Artaxates suggests the king announces a hunt as a distraction (6.3):

> δύνασαι γάρ, ὦ δέσποτα, σὺ μόνος κρατεῖν καὶ θεοῦ. ἄπαγε δὴ τὴν σεαυτοῦ
> ψυχὴν εἰς πάσας ἡδονάς. μάλιστα δὲ κυνηγεσίοις ἐξαιρέτως χαίρεις· οἶδα γάρ
> σε ὑφ' ἡδονῆς διημερεύοντα ἄβρωτον, ἄποτον.

> 'For you – and you alone – can master even a god; divert your own mind, then,
> with pleasures of all kinds. You are extremely fond of hunting in particular –
> indeed, I know you can go without food or drink all day when you are hunting,
> you like it so much' [trans. B.P. Reardon (1989)].

Artaxates' praise for the king's ability to endure long periods of hunger and
thirst whilst hunting, is reminiscent of Xenophon's praise of Cyrus the Great's
rigorous hunting expeditions and ability to undergo long periods without food and
drink.[38] As discussed in the first chapter, the royal hunt demonstrated a king's
worthiness to rule and his control over the land and Greek authors were aware of the
royal hunt's ideological importance, using it as a barometer for judging effective
kingship. Conversely, Chariton uses the hunt to demonstrate Artaxerxes' *decreasing*
control over his own passion, and subsequently the loss of control over his subjects
and land, culminating with the Egyptian rebellion (6.8). Although Artaxerxes may
have previously demonstrated kingly qualities in the hunt, his licentiousness has now
caused him to forget the purpose of the royal hunt, and results in him undermining
his own kingly authority. This is demonstrated by the extravagant nature of his
excursion (6.4):

> Ταῦτα ἤρεσε καὶ θήρα κατηγγέλλετο μεγαλοπρεπής... πάντων δὲ ὄντων
> ἀξιοθεάτων διαπρεπέστατος ἦν αὐτὸς ὁ βασιλεύς. καθῆστο γὰρ ἵππῳ Νισαίῳ
> καλλίστῳ καὶ μεγίστῳ χρύσεον ἔχοντι χαλινόν, χρύσεα δὲ φάλαρα καὶ
> προμετωπίδια καὶ προστερνίδια· πορφύραν δὲ ἠμφίεστο Τυρίαν (τὸ δὲ ὕφασμα

Βαβυλώνιον) καὶ τιάραν ὑακινθινοβαφῆ· χρύσεον δὲ ἀκινάκην ὑπεζωσμένος δύο ἄκοντας ἐκράτει, καὶ φαρέτρα καὶ τόξον αὐτῷ παρήρτητο, Σηρῶν ἔργον πολυτελέστατον... ἤθελε δὲ σεμνὸς ὑπὸ Καλλιρόης ὁραθῆναι...

The King accepted the suggestion, and a magnificent hunt was proclaimed... Every one of them was a sight worth seeing, but the most spectacular was the king himself. He was riding a huge, magnificent Nisaean horse whose trappings – bits, cheekpieces, frontlet, breastpiece- were all of gold, and wearing a cloak of Tyrian purple, woven in Babylon, and his royal hat was dyed the colour of the hyacinth; he had a golden sword at his waist and carried two spears, and slung about him were a quiver and bow of the costliest Chinese workmanship... he wanted Callirhoe to see him... [trans. B.P. Reardon (1989)].

The excursion is an elaborate display of wealth and luxury, designed to attract the admiration of Callirhoe. Lloyd Llewellyn-Jones discusses the power and hierarchy of the gaze in the Persian Empire,[39] signalling the hunting excursion as the moment Artaxerxes shifts from being the absolute master of the gaze to its victim.[40] Achaemenid kings controlled the gaze of their subjects, hence treasonous individuals were often blinded, and royal women's high rank was emphasised by the avoidance of the public gaze. For this reason, Stateira remains within the palace and Rhodogyne is sent as a delegate to participate in the beauty contest against Callirhoe when she first arrives (5.3). But Chariton's novel enters the *seraglio,* the residence of the royal women, providing the reader with an intimate viewing of this restricted space. Chariton destabilises hierarchies and subverts the power of the gaze firstly by entering the *seraglio* and then by having Artaxerxes willingly invite the gaze upon himself. Achaemenid kings not only controlled the gaze of their subjects but also avoided it, remaining invisible where possible and expecting their subjects to avert their gaze away from them.[41] Therefore the fact Artaxerxes *wants* to be seen undermines his authority, presents a decadent Babylon and hints at Persia's decline as an imperial power.[42]

Effeminate Babylon: influential eunuchs and women

Chapter one highlighted recurring literary figures associated with Mesopotamian court-life and discussed the influence of Ctesias in establishing an image of femininity dominating in Babylon. Chariton continues this tradition, not only

---

[39] Llewellyn-Jones (2013b), 167-191.
[40] Llewellyn-Jones (2013b), 176-177.
[41] Llewellyn-Jones (2013b), 173-7.
[42] Llewellyn-Jones (2013b), 169-171.

presenting Artaxerxes as a weak king but also depicting eunuchs and women as influencing the political sphere.

After the eunuch Artaxates suggests a legal loophole which would enable the king to pursue Callirhoe without fear of retribution, Artaxerxes recalls the hunt and returns to the palace in high spirits 'as if he had caught the finest game' (6.4).This invites a re-reading of the hunt as an erotic metaphor, in which the target of Artaxerxes' hunt is not game nor lions, but Callirhoe herself. The use of hunting imagery suggests Callirhoe is in a perilous and dangerous situation. Initially, Artaxerxes attempts to seduce her and sends Artaxates to pursue. The eunuch was delighted to undertake the task, believing it would be simple matter and would solidify his influence within the court. Artaxates' influence with the king is reminiscent of Ctesias' Artoxares, and he displays a similar scheming and ambitious nature:

> καὶ Ἀρταξάτης δὲ ἔχαιρε νομίζων πρὸς ἡδονὴν
> ὑπηρεσίαν ὑπεσχῆσθαι, βραβεύσειν δὲ λοιπὸν ἅρμα βασιλικόν,
> χάριν εἰδότων ἀμφοτέρων αὐτῷ, Καλλιρόης δὲ μᾶλλον·
> ἔκρινε γὰρ τὴν πρᾶξιν ῥᾳδίαν, ὡς εὐνοῦχος, ὡς δοῦλος, ὡς
> βάρβαρος. οὐκ ᾔδει δὲ φρόνημα Ἑλληνικὸν εὐγενὲς καὶ μάλιστα τὸ
> Καλλιρόης τῆς σώφρονος καὶ φιλάνδρου.

> Artaxates was in high spirits too; he thought that he had undertaken a valuable service and would be holding the reigns at court from now on, since both would be grateful to him, especially Callirhoe. He judged that it would be an easy matter to handle; he was thinking like a eunuch, a slave, a barbarian. He did not know the spirit of a wellborn Greek – especially Callirhoe, chaste Callirhoe, who so loved her husband. [trans. B. P. Reardon (1989)].

However, Artaxates miscalculates the difficulty of the task. The description of Artaxates as a eunuch, slave and barbarian presents him as embodying distinctly anti-Greek characteristics. This explains his inability to comprehend the fidelity of Callirhoe, whom he expected to readily accept the king's advances. Artaxates' non-Greekness is further exaggerated by his use of Mesopotamian rhetoric in his attempt to persuade Callirhoe that the king's desire is a great honour. The eunuch asks Callirhoe what her current husband(s) can offer her, and asks 'what fertile land do you own?'. As discussed in the first chapter, the fecundity of the land was considered a demonstration of divinely-ordained power. Artaxates' comment was a boast designed to demonstrate the power of the king compared to Callirhoe's husband(s). Callirrhoe's response not only surprises Artaxates, but also the reader, who is aware of Callirhoe's inner psyche. In the first chapter we saw how Babylon enhanced the violent capabilities of women. Callirhoe's response to Artaxates' reporting the king's desires suggests the city is beginning to influence her behaviour (6.5).

> Καλλιρόη δὲ τὸ μὲν πρῶτον ὥρμησεν, εἰ δυνατόν, καὶ
> τοὺς ὀφθαλμοὺς ἐξορύξαι τοῦ διαφθείροντος αὐτήν, οἷα δὲ
> γυνὴ πεπαιδευμένη καὶ φρενήρης, ταχέως λογισαμένη καὶ τὸν
> τόπον καὶ τίς ἐστιν αὐτὴ καὶ τίς ὁ λέγων, τὴν ὀργὴν μετέβαλε
> καὶ κατειρωνεύσατο λοιπὸν τοῦ βαρβάρου.

> Callirhoe's first impulse was to dig her nails into the eyes of this would-be pimp and tear them out if she could; but being a well-brought-up and sensible woman, she quickly remembered where she was, who she was, and who it was who was talking to her. She controlled her anger and from that point spoke hypocritically to the barbarian. [trans. B. P. Reardon (1989)].

Callirhoe's violent impulse is perhaps a consequence of being in Babylon. The characterisation of Artaxates, and Callirhoe referral to the eunuch as a 'barbarian' reiterates the non-Greek nature of the city. The passage shows Callirhoe's Greekness being tested, and for a brief moment she forgets her Greek-nature, almost resorting to violence and becoming a barbarian herself.[43]

On the second occasion Artaxates approaches Callirhoe, the danger is explicit. Artaxates reveals that the king wishes Callirhoe to consent, but he is prepared to use force to satisfy his lust (6.7). Throughout the novel, Callirhoe's beauty causes men to act uncontrollably: Dionysius is driven to the point of suicide (3.1) and Mithridates faints upon seeing her (4.1),[44] but it is the king, the very figure meant to preside over the law and maintain order, who displays the least control. Babylon marks the place where Callirhoe's chastity is most threatened; it is the point in the narrative where Chaereas and Callirhoe face their biggest obstacle yet, and the rather precarious situation hints at tragic ending. However, the Egyptian rebellion occurs and once Artaxerxes departs Babylon he diverts his attention away from

---

[43] According to Stephens (2008), 62 a common feature of the ancient novel is the Greekness of the protagonists being after leave their native shores and "are deprived of their accustomed status through misfortune, and have to negotiate dangerous circumstances and unfamiliar behaviour".
[44] Llewellyn-Jones (2013b), 178.

Callirhoe, enabling him to concentrate on his kingly duties and defeat the Egyptian rebellion. This suggests that there is some connection between being in Babylon and the king's licentious behaviour: when he is in the city his actions are determined by Callirhoe, but once he leaves, he is able to regain an element of self-control.

Chariton continues this tradition, depicting Babylon as a highly-eroticised space in which the king lacks control over his own passions, endangering his authority and threatening to derail the novel's happy conclusion. As we shall now see in the next section, Iamblichus depicts a similar image of Babylon but also incorporates elements of magic to present Babylon as a wondrous, treacherous space where nothing is quite as it seems.

Iamblichus' *Babyloniaka*

No other Greek text better encapsulates all the strands associated with Babylon, combining the eroticism, danger and magic, than Iamblichus' *Babyloniaka*. The fourth-century CE medical writer Theodorus Priscianus recommended Iamblichus' novel as a stimulant for those suffering sexual impotence, suggesting it was a highly-eroticised text.[45] In several respects, Iamblichus' *Babyloniaka* is a provocative novel due to its heavy emphasis on macabre events, its entirely Babylonian setting and the almost parodically dense concentration of novelistic *topoi* (in particular *Scheintod*, attempted suicide and escape from execution).[46] It is a novel of extremities and Iamblichus' presentation of the Babylonian king Garmus verges on caricature: he is licentious, remains within the confines of his palace in the company of eunuchs, and does not hunt nor fight. Garmus horrifically mutilates and punishes anyone who impedes his pursuit of Sinonis: the eunuchs Damas and Sacas have their ears and noses cut off (74a9), Damas is put to death (77a14), the goldsmith is slain, and the men who failed to guard Sinonis are buried alive alongside their wives and children (77a24). Garmus is an extreme version of the

---

[45] Theodorius, *Euporiston* 2.11 cites Iamblichus, Philip of Amphipolis and Herodian as cures for importance. See Stephens and Winkler (1995), 476 for translation of relevant passage.
[46] For attempted suicide see: Photius, *Bib. Codex 94* 75a.7 (Sinonis and Rhodanes poison); 75a.7 (Sinonis sword); 77a.14 (Rhodanes); 77b.18 (Rhodanes and Soraechus). For characters avoiding execution see: 74a.2 (Rhodanes crucifixion); 77b.20 (Euphrates and Mesopotamia avoiding beheading) and 78a.21-22 (Soraechus and Rhodanes avoiding crucifixion).

licentious despot, inflicting shocking violence onto his subjects and possessing no redeemable qualities.

Similar to Chariton's Artaxerxes, Garmus' obsession over the novel's heroine leads to the negligence of his kingly duties and undermines his authority.[47] Garmus' increasing lack of control is demonstrated by the disobedience of the eunuch Zobaras:

Καὶ διαγνοὺς ὁ Γάρμος μὴ εἶναι Σινωνίδα τὴν Μεσοποταμίαν, δίδωσι Ζοβάρᾳ παρὰ ποταμὸν Εὐφράτην καρατομῆσαι ἵνα μή, φησί, καὶ ἑτέρα τις τοῦ τῆς Σινωνίδος ἐπιβατεύσῃ ὀνόματος.
Ὁ δὲ Ζοβάρας ἀπὸ πηγῆς ἐρωτικῆς πιὼν καὶ τῷ Μεσοποταμίας ἔρωτι σχεθείς ,σῴζει τε ταύτην καὶ πρὸς Βερενίκην Αἰγυπτίων ἤδη, ἅτε τοῦ πατρὸς τελευτήσ αντος βασιλεύουσαν, ἐξ ἧς ἦν καὶ ἀφελόμενος, ἄγει· καὶ γάμους Μεσοποταμίας ἡ Βερενίκη ποιεῖται, καὶ πόλεμος δι' αὐτὴν Γάρμῳ καὶ Βερενίκῃ διαπειλεῖται.

[77b27] Garmos recognises that Mesopotamia is not Sinonis and gives her to Zobaras to have her beheaded by the river Euphrates, saying, "So that no other woman will take on herself the name of Sinonis." Zobaras, having drunk deep from the wellspring of passion and falling in love with Mesopotamia, rescues her. He departs to Berenike, who is now queen of Egypt after her father's death, and takes Mesopotamia with him. Berenike celebrates Mesopotamia's marriage, and because of Mesopotamia war is threatened between Garmos and Berenike. [trans. Stephens & Winkler (1995)].

As discussed in the first chapter, scheming and disloyal eunuchs feature associated with Mesopotamian courts since the Classical period. These eunuchs were depicted as calculating and instigated or supported plots due to their own political ambition. However, in Iamblichus' novel, Zobaras' disobedience is an impulsive act and the product of his own passion. Iamblichus' Babylon is such an erotically-charged space that even eunuchs, like Zobaras, exhibit sexual desire. It is uncertain whether Mesopotamia proceeds to marry Zobaras or the Egyptian Queen Berenice. An earlier narrative digression on Berenice's 'unnatural passion' (77a20)

---

[47] Frag. 1 describes an elaborate procession with numerous similarities similar to Chariton's hunting excursion. Although Iamblichus' king appears to be inviting the gaze upon himself, the procession is not a hunting excursion, but appears to be celebratory. There is debate over the nature of the procession, where it would fit in the novel and whether the king is Garmus or Rhodanes. Without knowing these details for certain we cannot determine whether the fragment is undermining the king's authority in a similar manner to Chariton's Artaxerxes. See Schneider-Menzel (1948), 68; Stephens and Winkler (1995), 222-3. All fragments follow the numbering of Stephens and Winkler (1995).

implies that a female homoerotic relationship existed between Berenice and Mesopotamia. In either scenario, Mesopotamia's marriage to either a woman or a eunuch, would subvert Greek socio-cultural norms and enhance the erotic intrigue of Iamblichus' novel.

Iamblichus' *Babyloniaka* is a novel which challenges boundaries, whether Graeco-Roman socio-cultural norms or the boundaries of its genre.[48] We may view the novel's Babylonian setting and non-Greek cast of characters as part of its flouting of convention. Whereas Chariton's novel only briefly enters Babylon, Iamblichus' novel takes place entirely within the Babylonian region, the only exceptions being Mesopotamia's flight to Egypt, and possibly Sinonis' marriage to the Syrian king. This is perhaps why Garmus loses his kingdom: unlike Chariton's Artaxerxes, Garmus sends Rhodanes to fight the Syrian king on his behalf, which proves catastrophic as Rhodanes ends up displacing Garmus as king. If Garmus had left the royal confines of Babylon (like Chariton's Artaxerxes) he may have regained control and consolidated his kingdom. The Babylonian setting also explains Sinonis' vengeful and violent behaviour. It was unusual for novelistic heroines to inflict violence upon themselves or others, but Sinonis demonstrates the capability to do both.

Violent women

After the magistrate Soraechus arrests Sinonis and Rhodanes for grave robbing, Sinonis persistently attempts suicide, stabbing herself in the process (75a16-75a30). Sinonis' actions impress Soraechus so much that he frees the couple and takes them to the Island of Aphrodite so that Sinonis can receive medical attention. Although Sinonis' attempted suicide was unusual it was not unique. We have already seen how in Xenophon *Cyropaiedea*, a proto-novelistic text, Panthea commits suicide by stabbing herself with a dagger.[49] In the fragmentary novel *Kalligone*, in an episode that is set in Scythia, we find a novelistic heroine attempting to kill herself. The exact cause of Kalligone's distress is uncertain but it revolves

---

[48] For example, the marriage of Mesopotamia, either to a woman or a eunuch; the excessive violence directed from the king as opposed to bandits who are normally responsible for violence in the ancient novel; slaves crossing acceptable boundaries, either by sleeping with their master's wife (fr.35) or in committing murder (76b10). See Morales (2006) for a discussion on these features.

[49] Xen *Cyr.* 7.3.14-5.

around her passion for Eraseinos. Kalligone reproaches her companion Eubiotos for removing her dagger and preventing her from committing suicide, threatening to murder him if he does not return her sword.[50] In terms of passionate anger and the threatening of others, only Sinonis matches Kalligone among the novel heroines.[51] After discovering that Rhodanes has kissed the farm-girl, Sinonis embarks upon a murderous rampage:

> Ῥοδάνης ἀπιὼν ἐφ' ᾧ φεύγειν φιλεῖ τὴν κόρην τοῦ γεωργοῦ, καὶ
> ἀνάπτεται εἰς ὀργὴν Σινωνὶς διὰ τοῦτο, εἰς ὑπόνοιαν μὲν πρῶτον
> ἀφιγμένη τοῦ φιλήματος, ἔπειτα καὶ ἀπὸ τῶν τοῦ Ῥοδάνους χειλέων
> ἀφελομένη τὸ αἷμα, ὃ φιλήσας αὐτὴν περιεκέχριστο, εἰς ἰσχυρὰν
> πίστιν καταστᾶσα. Ζητεῖ διὰ τοῦτο Σινωνὶς τὴν κόρην ἀνελεῖν,
> καὶ ὑποστρέφειν πρὸς αὐτὴν ἠπείγετο καθάπερ τις ἐμμανής·
> καὶ συνέπεται Σόραιχος, ἐπεὶ μὴ κατασχεῖν τῆς μανιώδους ὁρμῆς ἴσχυε.
> Καὶ καταίρουσιν εἰς πλουσίου τινός, τὸ ἦθος δὲ ἀκολάστου, Σήταπος
> αὐτῷ ὄνομα, ὃς ἐρᾷ τῆς Σινωνίδος καὶ πειρᾷ. Ἡ δὲ ἀντερᾶν ὑποκρίνεται,
> καὶ μεθυσθέντα τὸν Σήταπον κατ' αὐτὴν τὴν νύκτα καὶ τὴν ἀρχὴν τοῦ ἔρωτος
> ἀναιρεῖ ξίφει. Καὶ ἀνοῖξαι κελεύσασα τὴν αὔλιον, καὶ τὸν Σόραιχον ἀγνοοῦντα
> τὸ πραχθὲν καταλιποῦσα, ἐπὶ τὴν τοῦ γεωργοῦ κόρην ἠλαύνετο.

> [76b22] Rhodanes on leaving for his escape kisses the farmer's daughter and Sinonis flares up in anger. At first she comes to suspect the kiss, and then, when she wipes from his lips the blood that had been smeared on him when he kissed her, her suspicions are confirmed. Sinonis therefore seeks to kill the girl: she violently turned on her like a madwoman. Soraichos then followed her, since he was unable to restrain her maniacal energy. [76b31] They lodge at the house of a rich man of dissolute character, whose name is Setapos. He falls in love with Sinonis and presses his suit. She pretends to love him in return, and on that very night at the beginning of their lovemaking when Setapos is quite drunk, she kills him with a sword. She asked that the courtyard door be opened and, leaving Soraichos behind in ignorance of her deed, she hastened towards the farmer's daughter… [trans. Stephens & Winkler (1995)].

Sinonis is the only known novelistic heroine to commit murder and seek to harm others. Callirhoe momentarily has a violent impulse against the eunuch Artaxates, as we have seen, but she manages to restrain herself, whereas Sinonis acts on her impulses and in the most serious manner. In murdering her host, Sinonis breaks the Greek code of *xenia,* a severe act of hubris. The murder of Setapos could

---

be excused a rash, uncharacteristic act, but a fragment attributed to Iamblichus suggests a lack of remorse from Sinonis:[52]

> ἡ δὲ μεστὴ μὲν ἦν καὶ τῆς ἔμπροσθεν ζηλοτυπίας, προσείληφε δὲ καὶ τὴν ἀπὸ τῆς πράξεως εὐτολμίαν· ὡς οὖν ἐλάβετο τῆς ὁδοῦ, "ὁ μὲν πρῶτος ἀγών", ἔφη, "διηγώνισται· ἐχώμεθα δὲ καὶ τοῦ δευτέρου· καὶ γὰρ ἐν καιρῷ γεγυμνάσμεθα."

> She was full of her former jealousy and she had also added to it the boldness that followed from her deed. So when she took to the road, she said, "The first contest has been fought through. Let us grapple with the second. For we have had a timely exercise". [trans. Stephens & Winkler (1995)].

Sinonis is instead emboldened following the murder of Setapos, considering it a dress-rehearsal for the main event the murder of the farm-girl. Sinonis' ruthlessness and disregard for *xenia* can perhaps be attributed to the fact she is Babylonian and not Greek. However, Soraechus, who is also presumably Babylonian, demonstrates respect for *xenia* and warns Sinonis about breaking it and insulting Zeus, the protector of hospitality.[53] Soraechus' rationality fails to deter Sinonis, who proceeds in her second attempt to murder the farm-girl.

Rhodanes prevents Sinonis committing the act, prompting Sinonis to proceed to curse Rhodanes and run away to marry the king of Syria (77b9). Again Iamblichus' heroine subverts expectations, and contrasts with the unyielding fidelity of the protagonists that is so central to the ancient novel. The only possible exception is Callirhoe, but her marriage to Dionysius is for the sake of her and Chaereas' unborn child. Conversely, Sinonis' marriage to the Syrian king is out of jealousy and spite towards Rhodanes. The consequences of Sinonis' actions are severe and influence the political landscape of Mesopotamian as war ensues between Syria and Babylon, resulting in the overthrow of Garmus and accession of Rhodanes as king. Sinonis is not a typical novelistic heroine but her vengeful and violent nature is typical behaviour of Babylonian women, especially Ctesias' Semiramis. Both women are capable of violence, luring men to their bed before murdering them,[54] both marry a Syrian king, both have a strong connection to Babylon and influence politics.

---

[52] Fragment 70 = Souda 2.504.27, s.v. ζηλοτυπία.
[53] Frag. 61 = Vaticanus Graecus rescriptus 73, folio 61-62.
[54] Semiramis would select soldiers most outstanding in beauty, sleep with them and then kill them (F 1b = Diodorus 2.13.4).

Magic and the supernatural in Babylon

In addition to depicting Babylon as a highly eroticised and violent space, Iamblichus draws upon the lore and magic associated with Babylon. Iamblichus' novel features numerous instances of *Scheintod*,[55] including an episode where soldiers mistake the protagonists for ghosts (74b31). Similar to Callirhoe in the courtroom, the soldiers only entertain the possibility of ghosts being present due to being in Babylon, a space where such wondrous activities can occur. But Iamblichus goes a step further than Chariton by actually including an instance of attempted necromancy. Tigris' mother performs a magic ceremony (75b16), which precedes a narrative digression on the skills of a *magos*. As a Mesopotamian and a woman, Tigris' mother certainly qualifies as a necromancer in the Greek imagination,[56] and when she sees Rhodanes, she believes her dead son had returned to life (75b41). In reality, the 'resurrection' of Tigris is merely an instance of mistaken identity. However, Iamblichus provides another episode of necromancy where the explanation for the apparent resurrection is less obvious. The episode begins when an old Chaldean man interrupts the funeral of a maiden (74b42):

> καὶ καταλαμβάνουσι κόρην ἐπὶ ταφὴν ἀγομένην, καὶ
> συρρέουσιν ἐπὶ τὴν θέαν καὶ Χαλδαῖος γέρων ἐπιστὰς
> κωλύει τὴν ταφήν, ἔμπνουν εἶναι τὴν κόρην ἔτι λέγων·
> καὶ ἐδείχθη οὕτω. Χρησμῳδεῖ δὲ καὶ τῷ Ῥοδάνει ὡς
> βασιλεύσοι.

> 'Now they come upon a maiden being carried to the grave and they mingle with the crowd attending the spectacle. An old Chaldaian man stands up and forbids the burial, saying the maiden is still alive and breathing – and she was shown to be so. He also prophesises to Rhodanes that he will be king' [trans. Winkler & Stephens (1995)].

The Chaldean's role in this episode is twofold. Firstly, he appears to 're-animate' the corpse of the maiden. Chaldeans perform a similar role in Lucian' *Philopseudes* (11-13) and Lucian's *Menippus*[57] suggesting that by the second century

---

[55] Photius *Bib. Codex 94* 74b12 (Rhodanes and Sinonis honey); 75a8 (Rhodanes and Sinonis tomb) 77a29 (Sinonis and dog).
[56] As discussed in chapter two, Graeco-Roman literature tended to locate necromancers to the margins of the world (including Babylon in the East) and many practitioners were female. See Ogden (2001), 138.
[57] Cf. Philostratus, *Apollonius* 4.45 where Apollonius miraculously awakes a bride who appeared to be dead.

CE they had become affiliated with necromantic practices, at least, in the Greek comedic and novelistic tradition.[58] The second role the Chaldean fulfils is accurately predicting Rhodanes will become king. Chaldeans' association with (astrological) divination can be traced to Ctesias' *Persica*, in which they encourage rebellions through prophesising the overthrow of kings.[59] It is uncertain whether Iamblichus' Chaldean's prediction encouraged Rhodanes' kingly ambitions and his decision to rebel against Garmus, but by the end of the novel the Chaldean's prophecy is fulfilled.

Iamblichus' *Babyloniaka* reaffirms the Greek (and Roman) preconception of Chaldeans as highly-skilled (and potentially dangerous) in divination. Iamblichus even presented himself as learned in magic and skilled in divination, presumably astrological divination (75b27):

λέγει δὲ καὶ ἑαυτὸν Βαβυλώνιον εἶναι ὁ συγγραφεύς, καὶ μαθεῖν τὴν μαγικήν, μαθεῖν δὲ καὶ τὴν Ἑλληνικὴν παιδείαν, καὶ ἀκμάζειν ἐπὶ Σοαίμου τοῦ Ἀχαιμενίδου τοῦ Ἀρσακίδου, ὃς βασιλεὺς ἦν ἐκ πατέρων βασιλέων, γέγονε δὲ ὅμως καὶ τῆς συγκλήτου βουλῆς τῆς ἐν Ῥώμῃ, καὶ ὕπατος δέ, εἶτα καὶ βασιλεὺς πάλιν τῆς μεγάλης Ἀρμενίας. ἐπὶ τούτου γοῦν ἀκμάσαι φησὶν ἑαυτόν. Ῥωμαίων δὲ διαλαμβάνει βασιλεύειν Ἀντωνῖνον, καὶ ὅτε Ἀντωνῖνός, φησιν, Οὐῆρον τὸν αὐτοκράτορα καὶ ἀδελφὸν καὶ κηδεστὴν ἔπεμψε Βολογαίσῳ τῷ Παρθυαίῳ πολεμήσοντα, ὡς αὐτός τε προείποι καὶ τὸν πόλεμον, ὅτι γενήσεται, καὶ ὅποι τελευτήσοι. καὶ ὅτι Βολόγαισος μὲν ὑπὲρ τὸν Εὐφράτην καὶ Τίγριν ἔφυγεν, ἡ δὲ Παρθυαίων γῆ Ῥωμαίοις ὑπήκοος κατέστη.

'The writer says that he himself is a Babylonian and has learned magic, that he also had a Greek education, and that he flourished under Sohaimos the Achaimend and Arsakid, a king from a line of kings, and who became a member of the Senate at Rome and then a consul and then a king of Greater Armenia. This was the period in which he says he lived. He expressly states that Antoninus was ruling the Romans. And when Antoninus (he says) sent the emperor Verus, his brother and kinsman, to make war on Vologaeses the Parthian, he himself foretold that the war would occur and how it would end. And he tells how Vologaeses fled beyond the Euphrates and Tigris and how the land of the Parthians became subject to Rome.' [trans. Stephens & Winkler (1995)].

---

[58] Lucian, *Phil.* 11-13 recalls the tale of the Chaldean snake-blaster, in which a Chaldean revives a snake-bite victim before blasting all snakes present. See Ogden (2007), 65-104 for a commentary on tale of the Chaldean snake-blaster. According to Ogden (2008), 78 by the time of Alexander, the *Magi* had become conflated with Chaldeans.

[59] F 1pe* = Nicolas of Damascus (Konstantinos VII Porphyrogenetos, *Exc. de Insidiis* 3, p. 4.23 de Boor = FGrH 90 F3); F 8d* = Nicolas of Damascus (Konstantinos VII Porphyrogenetos, *Exc. de Insidiis* p. 23.23 de Boor = FGrH 90 F66).

There are a number of similarities between this passage and testimonia on Berossus, which suggests Iamblichus may have been imitating Berossus. Numerous ancient testimonies discuss the prophetic and astronomical skill of Berossus.[60] Iamblichus similarly establishes a Babylonian persona and presents himself as skilled in the power of prophecy, claiming he predicted the outcome of the Parthian War. Both Iamblichus and Berossus wrote Babylon-centric texts, and established a local, learned narrator to enhance their authenticity before engaging with Greek preconceptions of Babylon as a wondrous space. Iamblichus includes a narrative digression on the various types of magic that form the repertoire of the *magi* (75b16):

> Καὶ διεξέρχεται ὁ Ἰάμβλιχος μαγικῆς εἴδη,
> μάγον ἀκρίδων καὶ μάγον λεόντων καὶ μάγον μυῶν·
> ἐξ οὗ καλεῖσθαι καὶ τὰ μυστήρια ἀπὸ τῶν μυῶν
> (πρώτην γὰρ εἶναι τὴν τῶν μυῶν μαγικήν). Καὶ μάγον δὲ
> λέγει χαλάζης καὶ μάγον ὄφεων, καὶ νεκυομαντείας
> καὶ ἐγγαστρίμυθον, ὃν καί φησιν ὡς Ἕλληνες μὲν
> Εὐρυκλέα λέγουσι Βαβυλώνιοι δὲ Σάκχουραν ἀποκαλοῦσι.

'And Iamblichos goes through various types of skills of the *magos* – the *magos* who works with locusts and the *magos* of lions and the *magos* of mice, which is where the word "mystery" takes its name, from "mouse", for mouse-magic was the original type – and he says there is a *magos* of hail and a *magos* of serpents and of necromancy and a ventriloquist,[61] whom (as he says) the Greeks call Eurykles and the Babylonians Sacchouras' [trans. Stephens & Winkler (1995)].

This solidifies the narrator's status as learned in magic and as a purveyor of alien wisdom and also strengthens Babylon's association with magical practices. Iamblichus establishes an esoteric narrator learned in the knowledge he is transmitting, similar to Berossus' *Babyloniaka* and Lucian's *De Dea Syria*, which we explored in the second chapter. Although these texts all establish esoteric narrators, the genre of these texts impact on how Babylon/ Mesopotamia is presented. The historiographical approach of *De Dea Syria* is closer to the Herodotean tradition of Ionian inquiry and rationality, than it is to Iamblichus' novelistic approach which appeals to travel and exoticism. Thus, *De Dea Syria* and Iamblichus' *Babyloniaka*

---

[60] T 3 680 *BNJ* = Josephus, *App.* 1.128-131; T 5a 680 *BNJ* = Virtuvius Pollio, *On Architecture* 9.6.2; T 6 680 *BNJ* = Pliny, *NH* 7.123; T 7a 680 *BNJ* = Pausanias 10.12.9.

[61] Winkler (1985), 267 argues that Iamblichus' narrative digression on the types of *magos* deliberately mentions a ventriloquist to remind us that the entire story derived from a Babylonian learned in barbarian wisdom.

provide different lenses through which Mesopotamia is 'read'. Therefore, whereas Iamblichus uses his *persona* to reinforce Mesopotamia's association with magic, the narrator of *De Dea Syria* corrects certain misinformed Greek traditions regarding the origins and practices of Syria.

Iamblichus' novel also involves an additional stage of transmission, with Iamblichus claiming he heard the tale from a Mesopotamian prisoner of war. According to a scholion in Photius, Iamblichus' tutor was a Babylonian wise man who had been a prisoner of war under the Emperor Trajan:[62]

> οὗτος ὁ Ἰάμβλιχος Σύρος ἦν γένος πατρόθεν καὶ μητρόθεν, Σύρος δὲ οὐχὶ τῶν ἐπῳκηκότων τὴν Συρίαν Ἑλλήνων, ἀλλὰ τῶν αὐτοχθόνων, γλῶσσαν δὲ εἰδὼς καὶ <ἐν> τοῖς ἐκείνων ἔθεσι ζῶν ἕως αὐτὸν τροφεύς, ὡς αὐτός φησι, Βαβυλώνιος λαβών, Βαβυλωνίαν τε γλῶσσαν καὶ ἤθη καὶ λόγους μετεδιδάσκει, ὧν ἕνα τῶν λόγων εἶναί, φησι, ὃν καὶ νῦν ἀναγράφει. αἰχμαλωτισθῆναι δὲ τὸν Βαβυλώνιον καθ' ὃν καιρὸν Τραιανὸς εἰσέβαλεν εἰς Βαβυλῶνα, καὶ πραθῆναι Σύρ[ῳ] ὑπὸ τῶν λαφυροπώλων. εἶναι δὲ τοῦτον σοφὸν τὴν βάρβαρον σοφίαν ὡς καὶ τῶν βασιλέως γραμματέων ἐν τῇ πατρίδι διάγοντα γεγενῆσθαι. ὁ μὲν οὖν Ἰάμβλιχος οὗτος Σύραν τὴν [καὶ] πάτριον γλῶσσαν εἰδώς, ἐπιμαθὼν [καὶ] τὴν Βαβυλωνίαν μετὰ ταῦτα καὶ τὴν Ἑλληνά φησιν ἀσκῆσαι καὶ χρῆσι[ν] λαβεῖν ὡς ἀγαθὸς ῥήτωρ γένοιτο

> This Iamblichus was Syrian by birth on his father's and mother's side, but not a Syrian who was one of the Greeks who had settled in Syria, but one of the natives, who knew their language and lived according to their customs until a Babylonian tutor, as he himself says, took him and taught him instead the Babylonian language and habits and stories, and it is one of these stories, he says, which he is now recording. He says that the Babylonian was taken prisoner at the time when Trajan attacked Babylon, and that he was sold to a Syrian by the booty-sellers; and this man was learned in Babylonian learning so as even to have been one of the king's secretaries when he was in his own country. So this Iamblichus, knowing Syrian as his native language and then learning Babylonian as well says that later he also trained himself in Greek and excelled in its use so that he became a good rhetor. [trans. Bowie (forth.)].

According to this passage, it was from his Babylonian tutor, a former prisoner of war, that Iamblichus learned the *Babyloniaka*.[63] This provides a convenient strategy for accounting for the transmission of cultural knowledge in the text. But it also alludes

---

[62] *Marcianus graecus* 450.
[63] Bowie (forth.) highlights the similarities of pseudo-documentairsm in Iamblichus' *Babyloniaka* with Philostratus' *Apollonius*.

to the socio-political situation of Mesopotamia during Iamblichus' lifetime. A prisoner of war plays a significant role in the transmission of knowledge in the *Kyranides*, and like Iamblichus' tutor, he may also have been captured during Parthian war.[64] This inclusion of Mesopotamia/ Syrian prisoners of war in these texts reflects the instability of the region during the period, and is perhaps indicative of the suppression of Mesopotamian peoples under Roman imperial rule. Especially once we consider Iamblichus' own identity as a Syrian, writing about Babylon in Greek during the height of the Roman Empire, [65] we realise the complexities of cultural interaction during the period and the possible socio-political commentary Iamblichus' novel offers.[66]

A dangerous ecology: poisonous honey

Throughout Iamblichus presents Babylonia as a violent, dangerous and unstable region and this is epitomised in his depiction of poisonous honey. In the Roman world honey had a wide range of uses. It was used as a preservative, whether for food or corpses. Honey was also considered to be an aphrodisiac, and was used to sweeten food and medicine. It was a substance associated with life or preservation, but in Iamblichus' novel, honey causes pain and almost death.[67] Iamblichus' honey emphasises the treacherous nature of Babylon: it may appear to be one thing (a sweet preservative) but is in fact another (poisonous).[68] We encounter poisonous honey during a tense scene in which Garmus' men track Rhodanes and Sinonis to a cave. Garmus' men begin digging, at which point agitated bees attack them, enabling Rhodanes and Sinonis to escape:

> Καὶ μελιττῶν ἀγρίων σμήνη ἐκεῖθεν ἐπὶ τοὺς ὀρύσσοντας τρέπεται, καταρρεῖ δὲ τοῦ μέλιτος καὶ ἐπὶ τοὺς φεύγοντας· αἱ δὲ μέλισσαι καὶ τὸ μέλι ἐξ ἑρπετῶν πεφαρμακευμένα τροφῆς, αἱ μὲν κρούσασαι τοὺς ἐπὶ τὸ ὄρυγμα ἠκρωτηρίαζον, οὓς δὲ καὶ ἀπέκτειναν. Τῷ δὲ λιμῷ κρατούμενοι οἱ περὶ Ῥοδάνην διαλιχμησάμενοι καὶ τὰς γαστέρας καταρρυέντες, πίπτουσι παρὰ τὴν ὁδὸν ὡσεὶ νεκροί. φεύγουσιν ὁ στρατὸς τῷ τῶν μελισσῶν πολέμῳ

---

[64] Winkler (1985), 267-8. According to the *Souda s.v.* Ἰάμβλιχος, Iamblichus was himself a slave. Ἰάμβλιχος: οὗτος, ὥς φασιν, ἀπὸ δούλων ἦν. On the role of slavery in Iamblichus' *Babyloniaka* see Dowden (2019).

[65] See Millar (1993), 489-532 discusses the cultural interaction in the region during period.

[66] For political reading of Iamblichus' *Babyloniaka* see Morales (2006) who considers Mesopotamia, Tigris and Euphrates to embody the regions they are named after and views the numerous *Doppelgängers* as evidence of a lack of individuality and loss of cultural identity in Mesopotamia.

[67] Totelin (2017) discusses the use of honey in Greek medicine. She notes the deceptive nature of honey which tastes sweet but could conceal bitter substances.

[68] Totelin (2017), 71 considers 'one of the sweetest – but also at times controversial and dangerous – things a natural philosopher, agronomist or medical writer could produce was fine prose or poetry'.

πονούμενοι καὶ τοὺς περὶ Ῥοδάνην ὅμως διώκουσι, καὶ οὓς ἐδίωκον ὁρῶντες ἐρριμμένους παρέτρεχον, νεκρούς τινας ὡς ἀληθῶς ὑπολαμβάνοντες.
[*Bibl. cod.* 94, 74a40-74b5]

A swarm of wild bees from that place attacks the men digging, and some of their honey also drips onto the fugitives. The bees in fact have distilled their honey like a drug from the plants eaten by serpents: stinging the diggers, they mutilate some, others they actually kill.[69] Overcome by hunger, the party of Rhodanes licked up the honey, suffered stomach cramps and collapsed by the roadside like corpses. The army fled, hard pressed by the bee's warfare. And they were still pursuing the party of Rhodanes, and when they saw the persons they were pursuing lying by the road they rode on by, thinking they were in truth some corpses. [trans. Stephens & Winkler (1995)].

This fragment is attributed to Iamblichus which describes the honey as being gathered from snakes.[70] Catherine Connors suggests Iamblichus was drawing on Pliny the Elder.[71] Pliny describes poisonous honey as occurring from the *flos rhododendri* in the region of Sanni in Pontus (21.45).[72] Elsewhere, Pliny (16.33) describes *rhododendri* as a remedy for snake-bites, leading Connors to consider the possibility of a snake-summoning Mage living in the cave. Iamblichus' description of how the poisonous honey is produced is obscure; however his depiction of the potential side-effects of consuming the substance appears to adhere to other Greek accounts.

Xenophon' *Anabasis* (4.8.19-21) recalls an episode in which the Greek mercenaries consume poisonous honey whilst travelling through Colchis, east Pontus. The stomach cramps and fainting of the soldiers in Xenophon's account are reminiscent of the symptoms experienced by Rhodanes and his company in Iamblichus' *Babyloniaka*, which suggest Iamblichus aware of Xenophon's account. The reference to the 'bees' warfare' therefore is possibly alluding to Xenophon's account which describes the scene as looking like 'the aftermath of a defeat'. Iamblichus could also be alluding to Strabo. According to Strabo, during the

---

[69] Cf. Sandy (1989) translation: 'both the bees and honey are poisonous because the bees have fed on snakes'.

[70] Fr.16 in Habrich (1960). 'Since the honey was neither pure nor from acanthus but gathered from the nurturing of snakes it upset their insides' [trans. Connors (2017)].

[71] Connors (2017), 45.

[72] Pliny 21.44 also discusses a type of poisonous honey which occurs when bees feed on the plant *aigolethron* ('fatal to goats') at Heracleia in Pontus. See Connors (2017), 45.

Mithridatic Wars (88-63 BCE), King Mithridates of Pontus left a trail of poisonous honey pots for Pompey's army to find.[73] After eating the poisonous honey, the Roman army became disorientated and were slaughtered by the Persians, demonstrating the potentially fatal consequences of consuming poisonous honey.

For this reason, Greeks associated poisonous honey with their eastern neighbours. The Magi were considered experts in the medicinal and poisonous use of plants, which perhaps explains why Iamblichus' novel features poisonous honey.[74] The potential danger of plants is apparent once Rhodanes and Sinonis travel to an unnamed island sacred to Aphrodite, to seek treatment for Sinonis' self-inflicted stab wound. In a narrative digression, Iamblichus discusses the temple of Aphrodite and the priestess' three children; Tigris, Euphrates and Mesopotamia (75a36-75b16). It is revealed that Tigris died after eating a rose that had a cantharis hidden in it:

Ἐν δὲ τῇ προειρημένῃ νησῖδι ῥόδον ἐντραγὼν ὁ Τίγρις τελευτᾷ· κανθαρὶς γὰρ τοῖς τοῦ ῥόδου φύλλοις ἔτι συνεπτυγμένοις οὖσιν ὑπεκάθητο. Καὶ ἡ τοῦ παιδὸς μήτηρ ἥρωα πείθεται γενέσθαι τὸν υἱὸν ἐκμαγεύσασα. Καὶ διεξέρχεται ὁ Ἰάμβλιχος μαγικῆς εἴδη...

[75b16-20] On the aforementioned island, Tigris eats a rose and dies, for a blister beetle lurked in the folded petals of the rose. The boy's mother performs a magic ceremony and is convinced that he has become a hero. And Iamblichos goes through various types of skill of the *magos*... [trans. Stephens & Winkler (1995)].

According to Pliny (29.30) the cantharis bug was used to cure impotence but could also be deadly. The concealment of a cantharis bug within a rose growing on an island sacred to Aphrodite is full of sexual symbolism. There is also an element of word-play regarding the Greek word (rhod-), meaning rose. Rhod- the beginning of rhododendron, the plant which produces poisonous honey, and is also the beginning of Rhodanes' name. The episode appears to be warning about the dangers of love, at least erotic love. As aforementioned, *Scheintod* was a common motif of the ancient novel, but here we have a reversal of that trope in a case of mistaken

---

[73] Strabo 12.3.18.
[74] According to Ammianus 23.6.78, Persians do not touch anything when marching through enemy gardens through fear of poison and magical arts. See Connors (2017), 41 who discusses the Magi possible role in producing poisonous honey.

resurrection.[75] The misidentification happens because Rhodanes is the *Doppelgänger* of Tigris (as well as Euphrates). Whilst mistaken identity occurs in other ancient novels, nothing parallels the 'insistent duplicity of Iamblichus' comedy of errors'.[76]

In Babylon, appearances are deceptive and nothing is as it seems in Iamblichus' novel, with its murderous heroine, numerous *Doppelgängers* and many instances of *Scheintod.* Even the natural world is unpredictable and dangerous. Iamblichus' poisonous honey and deadly rose are emblematic of the erotic, dangerous and treacherous nature of Babylon.

Conclusion

From the Classical period Mesopotamian romances featured in Greek historiographical and biographical texts. These texts placed historical figures in romantic episodes and feature motifs that would become characteristic of the novels. This demonstrates that Mesopotamia was at the centre of the development of novelistic traditions, as a space where historiography and romance merged. The figures of Ninus and Semiramis demonstrate this, beginning as the legendary founders of the Assyrian Empire in Ctesias, before becoming a romanticised, and suitably Hellenized, couple in the Greek imagination during the imperial period. Chariton and Iamblichus engaged with pre-existing Greek traditions of Babylon, depicting a sensationalised court, featuring scheming eunuchs, weak, licentious kings and women capable of violence. Both authors present Babylon as a licentious space in which the chastity of the female protagonist is threatened by the king - the very figure meant to maintain control and order. Iamblichus' Babylon is such a highly-eroticised space it is even possible for eunuchs to fall in love and female homoerotic relationships to occur. Iamblichus is a novel of extremes, largely due to its Babylon setting. Whereas Chariton focuses on court intrigue, Iamblichus combines episodes of extreme violence with numerous episodes of magic. Iamblichus regularly subverts expectations of the novel to exaggerate the instability and danger of Babylon, which is encapsulated by the treacherous nature of flora and

---

[75] Kasprzyk (2017), 32.
[76] Morales (2006), 93.

fauna. In the city thresholds are slippery: whether the genre of a text, identity of characters, the dynamics of power, boundaries between life and death or the boundaries of realities, nothing is quite as it seems in Babylon.

CONCLUSION

This thesis has shown how certain practices and behaviours, initially associated with ancient Mesopotamia or the Achaemenid Empire, eventually became affiliated with Babylon as a city. Regardless of the rulers or occupants of Babylon, femininity dominates the characterisation in the form of effeminate kings, empowered royal women and influential eunuchs. In the first chapter I highlighted the significance of Ctesias in establishing Babylon's reputation as an effeminate city where traditional gender roles are regularly inverted. Babylon is repeatedly presented as a space which prompts involuntary transformation, such is the case in Ctesias' story of Nanarus and Parsondes, in which Parsondes' transformation is so great that he is misgendered. Similarly, later Hellenistic writings depict Alexander of Macedon as transformed and corrupted by Babylonian decadence. This thesis shows the continuation of this presentation in the ancient novel, as kings confined to Babylon exhibit licentious and despotic behaviour, which threatens their empire's stability, but once they leave the city (in the case of Chariton's Artaxerxes) they are capable of regaining control.

The first chapter also discussed how Greek authors used the royal hunt, an important Mesopotamian ideological tool, to determine the effectiveness of kingship: rulers who did not hunt were effeminate and weak, whilst those who participated in the hunt were effective and authoritative rulers. Similar to the hunt, royal gardens were likewise an important ideological tool demonstrating a Mesopotamian king's worthiness to rule and maintain control over his land. In the first chapter I show how the Greek admiration for Mesopotamian royal gardens influenced their very language – with the introduction of the term *paradeisos* – and their own garden design, whilst the Hanging Garden continued to captivate the Greek imagination even after Greek technology had surpassed that of the legendary garden. The Hanging Garden, along with all the wonder and lore it encapsulates, became (and remains) associated with Babylon.

In the second chapter I further addressed the wondrous nature of Babylon, focusing on the city's association with magical practices, particularly astrology and necromancy, and its reputation for ancient, esoteric knowledge. The chapter primarily discusses three texts written by non-Greek authors who each presented themselves as transmitting Mesopotamian/ Babylonian esoteric knowledge. The narrative devices employed by Berossus, Lucian and the *Kyranides* (mainly their citation of sources and the establishment of an esoteric narrator) enhanced the texts' credibility and in chapter three I show how Iamblichus employed similar devices. These texts demonstrate the continued Greek fascination with Babylon into the imperial period and enhanced its reputation as a wondrous space. I also argue, however, that they reflect cultural hybridity and hint at cultural suppression due to Roman imperialism, which is particularly evident in Lucian's anonymous narrator and the *Kyranides'* reliance on a Syrian prisoner of war for the transmission of knowledge.

In the final chapter I show how the numerous strands of the Greek imagination of Babylon combined in the ancient novel. The chapter explores how Mesopotamia was at the centre of developing novelistic traditions, as a space where historiography and romance merged and the boundaries between history and fiction became distorted, which is evident from proto-novels of Xenophon and Ctesias, and in the figures of Ninus and Semiramis. I argue that by the early imperial period specifically Babylonian, rather than Mesopotamian, romantic endeavours were popularised, which is demonstrated by the city's prominence in the ancient novels of Chariton and Iamblichus. The chapter highlights the multiple similarities between Chariton and Iamblichus' depiction of Babylon, with both authors: engaging with pre-existing Greek traditions of Babylon, presenting the city as a dangerous and licentious space, featuring recurring literary figures of weak kings, and including women capable of violence and scheming eunuchs. However, I argue that Iamblichus was more extreme in his presentation of Babylon, with his unredeemably cruel, despotic king, numerous macabre episodes (including a murderous heroine), a parodically high number of D*oppelgängers* and instances of *Scheintod*, the highly eroticised nature of his Babylon (which enables eunuchs to fall under its spell and female homoeroticism to occur), and his emphasis on the magical and wondrous aspects of Babylon (including multiple episodes of divination and necromancy). Iamblichus regularly subverts expectations of the novel to exaggerate the instability and danger of Babylon, which I demonstrate through my analysis on the dangerous ecology of his novel.

In Babylon, especially Iamblichus' Babylon, thresholds are slippery. Whether the genre of a text, the identity of characters, the dynamics of power, the boundaries between life and death or the boundaries of realities, nothing is quite as it seems. This thesis has shown how Babylon held a particularly special place in Greek imagination as a cultural and literary cross-roads: it was space symbolic of the cultural hybridity and suppression of the imperial period, but also a space capable of captivating the historical, scientific, magical and fictional imagination.

9 789971 671051